18 YEARS A SCREW

by John Crook

Chapters

SET ME LOOSE FROM THIS MADHOOSE

NO AFFECTION IN THE PROTECTION
SECTION

A QUANDARY IN THE LAUNDRY

HERE COMES MY FUTURE FOR ALICIA
TO BUTCHER

CROOKY THE ROOKIE Monday, July 1st 1985

I would be turning twenty-two the following day and had finished serving my time as an apprentice painter and decorator over a year before and suddenly I found myself standing in an enclosed stone-walled exercise yard wearing shiny boots and a uniform. I was surrounded by hundreds of angry-looking rough-shaven men all dressed in stripey shirts and washed-out jeans and they were all walking around in a large, anti-clockwise circle.

My application to join the Scottish Prison Service had been successful and I was working as a screw in 'the big hoose with the wee windies', Her Majesty's Prison, Barlinnie. The largest jail in Scotland and one of the oldest, and coldest too I would add. Glasgow's notorious Bar-L! The place just reeked of history and draconian oppressiveness. This was the 1980's and the era of the ice-cream wars, hunger strikes, heroin, dirty protests, hostages and rooftop riots! WELCOME TO BARLINNIE!

"What in the name of the wee man have you got yourself into now Crooky?" I began to ask myself.

I had wanted a career change from decorating as it wasn't what I had planned to do forever but this was surely kicking it up a notch? It was a baptism of fire like no other. Not really what I had in mind, but if it prevented me from being laid off work each year as a result of the wet winter weather then it will do, for now. In the decorating game it was always the same old story,

'I'm afraid we need to lay some of you guys off as we don't have enough work coming in.' was the usual caveat every November.

My best mate Gus said he had experienced the same brush off from *his* boss, 'Come back in the spring.' he was told, to which Gus replied, 'What do you think I am, a fuckin' daffodil?' forgetting that he might have to ask this dude for a reference in the future. Decorating had been a means to an end at the time but I wanted something that was steady and more or less redundancy proof.

One Saturday night over a few beers I got chatting to big Ray in the Chryston Tavern. He was a bit of a boozer and his nickname was *The Exorcist*. So-called because whenever he visited anyone's house, all the spirits would disappear!

Ray was a screw at Longriggend Remand Unit near Airdrie and he started telling me how his week at work had been.

Ray's week at work grabbed my attention immediately, as it seemed a lot more interesting than any week at work of mine had *ever* been; stripping wallpaper and glossing doors isn't exactly full of intrigue. I hadn't really given prisons, or prisoners for that matter, a second thought up until this point.

I quizzed Ray all night and left the pub fascinated by it all; if a wee bit intoxicated. Impulsively, a few days later, I was on the phone for an application form to join the Scottish Prison Service as a Prison Officer.

The entrance examination at that time was a series of multiple-choice general knowledge questions and psychometric type tests that I apparently passed with flying colours. This was followed a few weeks later by an interview, where three members of the senior management team fired off questions at the candidate and set up hypothetical situations for them to ponder and give their opinion on. Before I knew it I was seated on a chair in the middle of a large room inside the Staff Training Block with three suits behind a row of tables ten feet away, hitting me with scenarios such as,

'What would you do Mr Crook, if a prisoner threw a punch and it hit you square on the face?'

'Jesus wept!' I thought, 'is that a possibility?'

As I was pondering his question and attempting to formulate my answer, the second suit interrupted the silence with,

'Do you have any experience of violence and disruptive behaviour Mr Crook?'

I thought about saying, 'Sure, I went to Chryston High School and the Moodiesburn Young Team were a force to be reckoned with!' but I didn't think that this was the time or the place to be cracking a funny!

'I have broken up one or two fights in my time,' was my actual answer.

'Oh, so you like violence then?' He goads.

'No, I wouldn't say that I liked it, but I'm prepared to get involved if the situation requires it, or if someone needs help.' I retorted. Thinking that *that* was what he wanted to hear.

It was hard to know exactly what they were looking for and I suppose there are no bona fide correct answers. They only wanted to hear if you had an opinion and how you expressed it; how you reacted under a bit of pressure and stress was their primary objective. The last thing they wanted was an incompetent imbecile who froze at the slightest sign of trouble or who didn't have anything constructive to say. I guess that it didn't matter so much what you said, more how you said it.

Several months later, I discovered that the interview panel had already made up their mind about you before you even lifted your cheeks off the seat. If they felt that you had impressed them enough, you were taken to the hospital block for a medical immediately after the interview. Apparently when an applicant stood up to leave at the end of the interview, one of the suits would signal with his thumb like a Roman Emperor to the officer escorting them out, whether or not you were going for a medical or shown the big hoose's exit door. I had learned this from the staff-training officer's assistant Robbie Conn, who said he remembered me getting the thumbs up at my interview once I had started working alongside him. We were to subsequently work together on the second flat of 'A' Hall for a year and Robbie became a good friend.

'Do you have any family or friends who are already in the service Mr Crook?' one of the suits asked me.

'I know someone that works in Longriggend Remand Unit and he drinks in my local pub.' I answer with unease.

'Oh, so you like a good drink then do you?' another interjects. 'Er, not really, just occasionally on a Friday or Saturday night' I lied.

'Cheeky auld goat', I thought. I half expected to be quizzed on my weekly intake of alcohol units, but that system fortunately hadn't been devised at the time.

The interview must have gone well because directly afterwards I was duly taken to the hospital block where a medical examination was carried out. The elderly doctor asked me to take off my shoes and socks, jacket, shirt and trousers. I immediately thought, 'Will I need to do a fake cough while old Doctor Heckle here fondles my privates? Who cares, at least I might get a steady job and a non-contributory pension at the end of it all.'

He asks me if I have any tattoos as he looks inside my mouth and ears. I really don't know if he understood where tattoos were traditionally placed. 'No, I don't have any tattoos.' I answer. He then asks a series of other medical questions as he runs his hands up and down the back of my legs to check for varicose veins, he said.

I tell him that I'm a non-smoker with no problems medically. He then told me to make an appointment with my GP to arrange to have a mass radiography carried out. Once this came back clear, I should expect a date from the Scottish Home & Health Department to start work at a prison, 'The establishment at which you start may not necessarily be Barlinnie.' He informed me.

I was then escorted back to the main gate twenty minutes or so later for my release back into the outside world. I felt relieved that my ordeal was over. I could go home and prepare for an invitation to hopefully drop through my letterbox inviting me to start working as a screw with the prison service. With a bit of luck that would be soon, as I had been made redundant a few weeks earlier and fiscally, things were getting pretty grim.

I had recently been introduced to the delights of signing on the dole for the first time. The local decorating firm I'd been employed with called Transform had gone into liquidation and I had been forced to transform my finances. I even had to cut the £5 per week 'dig money' that I paid to my mother. Desperate times, so I did what Maggie Thatcher's then employment secretary Norman Tebbit had suggested I do at the time, I had got on my bike (metaphorically at least) and looked for a job; now I was just hoping that I had found one.

Five months later I held my breath as I tore open the much-awaited letter:

'The Director of The Scottish Prison Service has made the following order.' The heading stated.

Very officious and bureaucratic I thought.

'John Crook, you are required to be present at HMP Barlinnie at 9am on Monday the first of July 1985', etc., etc.

I had mixed emotions about it all now and felt an equal amount of excitement *and* apprehension as I thought, 'Oops!'

If I'm honest, given my self-esteem at that time, I never thought I was going to be offered the job so the realisation hit me like a hot steam iron in the face; I was going to be working in Barlinnie! That big gruesome, ancient looking black stone fortress that you can see from the Provanmill traffic lights, as you head up town for a Saturday night of revelry. I'd seen the massive soot-covered chimneys hundreds of times but hadn't thought anything about them except that they looked oppressive, I'd thought even less about the occupants. Now, a year or so later, I was excited at securing full time employment but uneasy at the prospect of working in the Bar-L.

That warm but menacing morning duly arrived and I left my parents' home in Chryston where I lived to catch the X39 Bluebird bus into Glasgow. The double-decker was deathly silent that morning as I sat at the front near Gerry the driver, staring out of the windscreen at the hazy road ahead. Gerry McLean was a local guy who knew me well and couldn't believe his ears when I told him where I was going.

'Fuck sake, Spider, you're going to be working as a screw in the Bar-L?'

Spider was my nickname at the time, on account of me having been a goalkeeper when I was at school and all arms and legs so no one could get the ball past me. I was beginning to wish I'd stuck in at being a 'keeper as I said farewell to Gerry several minutes later and jumped off his bus at Riddrie Library to make my way up the 300-yard driveway towards the entrance of the jail.

I turned the unremarkable handle of the unremarkable door and walked inside.

The first thing that had struck me about the place when I first poked my nose through the main entrance door for my interview five months earlier was the smell, and it hadn't changed any. This place smelled fishier than a fish's wet bits. It was a combination of disinfectant, cheesy socks, stale food and terror. Every older style prison that I have visited since has emitted the same rancid odour. If cockroaches have a scent then I'm guessing that they're what the main source is, because older jails were overrun with the wee feckers. On the night shift, if you switched on the lights in the pantry areas, you could see legions of cockroaches scuttling away under the heated storage trolleys.

Most prisons have a small vestibule area as you enter the exterior pedestrian door; it's normally around three metres by three metres or thereby, but the vestibule in Barlinnie was so big that it made you feel like you were actually inside the main prison already. There seemed to be officers and civilians everywhere, all doing their own autonomous tasks like the 'Borg collective' from Star Trek!

A couple of men in smart suits walked past me toward the exit, I struggle to guess who everyone might be. Those pair must be lawyers or something? Soft dark-brown leather folders tucked under their arms, clean shirts and ties and those suits weren't bought from George At ASDA either that's for sure. Two uniformed cops were standing over in a corner talking to a prison officer and I presume a prisoner in civilian clothing. The young fella looked like he was about to be released as he was carrying all of his worldly possessions in a large bag marked SPS. I extrapolate that he must be getting arrested as soon as he steps outside.

I wonder how often that occurs?

Quite a lot as it happens, it's called a Gate Arrest. How apt, I wonder how long it took them to make that truism up?? At least the cops know where they can pick the guy up without any risk of him getting away!

A prisoner around my age walked past me with a mop bucket and began to clean the entire ceramic tiled entrance area with pine-scented disinfectant. As if the place doesn't smell bad enough, I thought! I got chatting to him and he asked me if I'm, 'One of the eight new recruits that are starting this morning?'

I was rather impressed at his knowledge of the day's forthcoming events. He told me his name was Harry and that he was the gate 'passman' and his job was to keep the gate area clean and run any errands for the Governor and staff in the administration block.

Passmen are what you might term a 'Trusty', they're the last men to be locked up at night and their's are the first cells to be unlocked in the morning. They basically help officers carry out mundane and tedious tasks. Harry certainly had his finger on the pulse and I took to him instantly, he seemed to be the opposite from what I expected prisoners to be like. We all have preconceived ideas about people, if we're completely honest. Harry was so far removed from the troll-like character that I had created for him in my narrow-minded reality.

I watched him mopping around me as I stood there taking everything in, it all seemed to be happening in slo-mo. He certainly looked mean and had the kind of face that had worn out at least two bodies, the sort of guy who would rip your lungs out and feed them to his dog if you looked at him the wrong way. But in actual fact, Harry was as charming as any movie star and as funny as any comedian you could meet. I got to know him over the following months and he was an absolute gem, a true diamond in the rough!

THE OPINION FROM THIS MINION

I am aware some people hold the belief that prisoners are the 'scum of the earth' and that they 'deserve everything they get'. I have even had some friends and family say to me,

'How can you be pleasant to those guys in jail?'

What are my feelings on that? Well, here's my opinion, for what it's worth:

To carry out the job professionally and effectively, it is essential to develop good working relationships with inmates. This is fundamental, as it not only makes the job far more tolerable but you get so much more from people if you treat them with respect and humanity. It's not everyone who has the ability to act with impartiality and compassion though, especially when faced with what an inmate may have been convicted of.

However, prison staff are not chosen for their abilities to be '*Judge Judy*' and Executioner. The convicted have been punished; the Court has already handed down their sentence and that is the end of the matter. People who work with prisoners are merely custodians, employed to facilitate the needs and entitlements of their charges according to what the state has decreed. A large percentage of offenders and their families live in deprived areas and some have complex issues that, as a society, we frequently ignore to our shame and cost.

Nevertheless, I am aware that not everyone holds this view. I have witnessed inmates being spoken to, and treated, pretty harshly at times.

I remember one old screw in particular named Jack McGill; he was a pretty mean old bastard. I don't think I ever heard him speaking in a civil tone towards any prisoner. I would frequently hear him pass really snide and cruel remarks at them like,

'Yer maw wiz a Vax!' or 'Away and lie in yer kennel, ya prick!'

I suppose Jack thought he was being funny, which of course he wasn't and most of the cons that came across him, detested him. Some of the staff loathed him too such was his malevolent outlook on reality. He never had a good word to say about anyone and when working late shifts with him he'd get all nostalgic, telling stories through whisky-reeking breath about the good old days in the Bar-L when you could 'Kick fuck oot of them and get away wi it!'

He would complain that nowadays prison staff saw themselves as, "Social workers who wanted to talk to these lowlifes respectfully like they were normal people!"

Elizabeth Fry, start spinning now!!

'I'd give the cunts bread and water and maybe a spoonful of jam at Christmas if they're fuckin lucky!' he'd proudly proclaim and anyone not agreeing with him was one of those, 'ignorant liberal arseholes', as he dubbed them. His mental incapacity to comprehend the bottom line was mind-boggling.

I remember when a notorious Glasgow underworld figure was walking past us on his way to his cell and I asked Jack who the fella was.

"That's Wink MacDonald." He told me. "The cunt was causin' a bit of a rammy in here a few months ago and some of us were geein him a kickin and I jumped aff the fourth step of that staircase right onto his heid!" Jack added with venom.

I had been in the job a matter of weeks at that point and began to wonder if I'd made a huge mistake? It was screws like Jack that made the job for everyone else that wee bit more difficult and dangerous. What I mean is he gave every decent screw, of which I have met more than plenty, a really bad name and further tarnished the already stained image of prison officers; reducing them to the stereotype we often see on TV of prison staff being brutal, hard-hearted half-wits. Jack McGill and all those right-wing dinosaurs like him were beginning to make me feel embarrassed about what I did for a living. I was reluctant to tell people that I was a prison officer; instead, telling anyone who asked that I worked for the Civil Service; which was technically true.

It has been suggested that being less aggressive with prisoners may lead to staff being treated with contempt. On the contrary, instead of prison officers treating prisoners the way Jack McGill did, I actually found that when I went out of my way to be respectful towards them regardless of their demeanour, prisoners as human beings found it difficult to be anything other than respectful back. Monkey see, monkey do and all that.

It didn't surprise me that some prisoners were still sceptical of this new approach from the recent intakes of staff, who now showed a degree of compassion and placed a wee bit more emphasis on care rather than merely containment. It is an extraordinary concept spending your working life with people who loathe what you represent, but never envisage just how different their incarceration could be without your involvement in it.

The latest information I heard regarding the 'phenomenon' that was officer Jack McGill; he had been charged with stealing from a bookies shop in Glasgow and after a short spell behind bars himself, languished as a penniless alcoholic, bedridden and receiving specialist care in a home. Funny that. Some might say ironic, almost.

Meanwhile back at Barlinnie vestibule and waiting to be 'inducted' into the job. I strode over to the green-tinted window of the gatehouse and handed the officer behind the three-inch bullet-resistant glass, my letter of employment through the security hatch.

As he reads the letter, I look over his shoulder and into the darkened room behind him. There is an array of television screens and panels with flashing lights, different coloured buttons and switches of varying sizes and designs. There are officers all placed at different strategic stations and it looks like organised mayhem in there. Phones are constantly ringing and radios are crackling with static and I count at least half a dozen staff. I then notice the name EDDIE STOBART in huge letters reflected in the glass.

WHAT?? 'Where the hell is that?' I thought.

It was an articulated truck sitting in the vehicle lock, which was on the opposite side of the pedestrian entrance. This place is enormous! Eddie Stobart must have made a fortune from crime as his trucks were never out of the Bar-L delivering supplies, from inmates' food to all kinds of raw materials.

Whenever any car, bus, truck or delivery van leaves or enters the prison they must drive through the vehicle lock first, passing the 25-foot high electronic gate before it slides shut behind them. They are then thoroughly searched by gate staff and processed before being allowed through the 2nd gate. This system isn't airtight and a few escapes have been made through here.

One brave but very lucky prisoner had previously hidden up inside the wheel arch of a large HGV truck as it prepared to leave through the vehicle lock. Luckily he was spotted and removed, as the consequences of him losing his grip and falling into the spinning wheel of the truck, are pretty horrific. I remember another escape through the vehicle lock, which was successful if only for a short while.

A large laundry van was due to leave one morning and in the back hidden under dozens of canvas bags was a notorious veteran escaper. I can only assume that it was a busy day because it wasn't properly searched and he was able to slide the metal shutter up and jump out of the back of the van at the traffic lights on Cumbernauld Road.

Ditching his stripey prison uniform for a pair of white shorts and a vest, '118 style', he started running along the main road like he was in training for a local half marathon run, ingenious! The cops picked him up a few days later though, and the search procedures at Barlinnie gate were tightened up a bit!

In the meantime I'm still standing at the glass window waiting like a dummy, when one of the gate officers passed my letter back through to me. He pointed the way up the staircase to my right and into the admin block where a crabbit old chief officer in a white shirt and with a big red strawberry for a nose, was waiting for me.

'I'm Chief Officer Sillars,' he announces, 'Just follow me.'

I walked slightly behind him down the long corridor as he growled something inaudible to the human ear. The Chief then showed me into a room where a further seven 'fresh out of the polythene' screws were sitting getting to know each other. These guys were my fellow new recruits and we would spend the next year together in training at Barlinnie and at the prison service college in Polmont.

Four of them were ex-forces and had apparently been advised to consider the prison service as a career option when they were being demobbed. Another two had worked for the SPS as civilians at H.Q. and the last one, a lovely guy named Frank Main, was the son of an officer that had worked at Barlinnie for thirty years. I felt like I was the only outsider, an infiltrator who had slipped through the mesh. One of the guys asked me where I had worked previously.

'I was a decorator.' I answered, slightly ashamed that my credentials weren't quite as fitting to this new post as all of their's appeared to be.

Thankfully most of them turned out to be top blokes and we got on really well. I did find it highly amusing though that every single one of them had a moustache except me! It turned out that most screws that had started recently had moustaches; it seemed to be fashionable at the time, well it was the eighties after all. When I arrived in 'A' Hall for my first day after training, '*Bootsie*' McMahon the Principal Officer (P.O.) in charge of the shift asked me,

'Where's your moustache, young man?'

I smiled and joked that I hadn't been issued with one on my arrival at the uniform store. Bootsie then rummaged around frantically in the desk drawer whilst asking all of his staff what they had done with the new rookie's moustache!

Incidentally one of those rookies on my course, an ex-squaddie named John Crossan, was ultimately to be taken hostage during a riot where he was seen on television being dragged onto the roof at Peterhead Prison like a POW only eighteen months later. I'm sure if he had known that this was about to happen, he would have chosen to remain at Barlinnie, or better still, safely back in the Army!

We were taken to the Staff Training Block where we met our new gaffer, a pleasant P.O. named Alec Peden. He was in his late forties and we stuck to him like limpets whenever he took us anywhere.

First off, he took the other lucky seven and myself to be kitted out with uniforms. We had each previously filled in a form with our sizes and the apparel was waiting for us to collect from the stores.

Jackets, Trousers, Shirts, Belts, Caps, Badges, Boots, the lot. I had written my hat size as a seven and three-quarters because I hadn't worn a cap since I was a cub-scout and hadn't a clue what size I was, so I just made it up. The hat ended up hanging down over my ears like oor Wullie's bucket. Luckily for me, fellow rookie Paul Stevenson's hat was far too small for him, so we swapped. Paul then earned the nickname 'Heid' because of the gargantuan size of his hat. In fact, nobody had a uniform that fitted properly, we were stood there looking like eight sacks of potatoes, each tied in the middle with an old piece of rope.

Every day we were taken to the gym for several hours of 'Control & Restraint' training, which is loosely based on mixed martial arts and consisted of various holds and wrist locks. These were designed for defence purposes and rarely used in reality by myself if I'm completely honest.

Each of us recruits was assigned a division, four on the 1st division and four on the 2nd. Having two divisions ensured that the prison, which had been running the same way for over a century, operated smoothly and without a hitch, well mostly. There was the occasional mishap with the rosters but not often and certainly not major. This place had been a prison since the mid 19th century so the regime was well established and ran like a slick, oiled machine. It had to. While division one were working a week of early shifts, division two would be on a week of back shifts. Each division was on duty on alternate weekends. Nightshifts were rare, around two weeks per year as there were only a handful of officers required on duty, given that the prisoners were all tucked up in their bunks behind a heavy-duty cell door all night.

All eight of us rookie turnkeys were rostered to work our first two weeks Monday to Friday on a 9am until 5pm dayshift as a sort of taster of prison life. We would spend a few hours a day observing and taking notes in each different area of the jail. Reception, Visit Room, Gate Lodge, etc., they called it an induction period. Then those of us assigned to division one had a week working from 1pm until 9:30pm late shift, with a 6am until 2:30pm early shift on the following week. I had spent these first four weeks under the supervision of P.O. Alec Peden and then a further six weeks residential training course at the prison service college at Polmont, near Falkirk. Once I was back working at Barlinnie and on the staff complement, I would be a fully-fledged 'Soldier of the State'; well, after my one years' probation was successfully completed, I would be.

If you messed up you were out on your ear though as a few who had gone before me had found to their eternal shame, with one Barlinnie officer having been sentenced to six years for smuggling drugs into the jail.

Ouch!

SMUGGLING DRUGS FOR ALL THE MUGS

The six weeks residential at the Prison College in Polmont near Falkirk was a strange experience and one for which I had no previous frame of reference. Recruits had their own single room much like a cell, ironically, but a slightly more deluxe version; bars on the windows nonetheless. My training course was males only, 29 of us to be precise so no extracurricular conjugal activity took place during my six-week stay at 'Chez Polmont'; well, not that I was aware of and certainly not by myself.

The recruits came from jails all over Scotland and had started working at their particular establishments on the same day as me. Occasionally there were several female recruits on these 'initial training' courses and from these groups wee couples would often blossom. Management didn't like to encourage this frivolous recreational diversion however, so staff had to be cautious about anything that they may have got up to with the other recruits. The last thing you wanted was to be dragged in front of the Chief Officer accused of messing about with a fellow employee; or you could both find yourself being sent home faster than you could shout, 'Slop Out!'

Every morning we were taken outside to the parade ground for an hour or so of 'square bashing'. This was something I hadn't done since the Boys Brigade and I treated it with light-hearted banter, it was the only way to get through it.

The SPS was deemed to be one of those disciplined occupations like the Police and Fire services and that was why this military-styled regimen was included in the training curriculum. I remember one of the Chief lecturers telling us on our first day that, by the end of the course we wouldn't know whether our 'arses had been punched, bored or countersunk!' I was a bit alarmed by this announcement but I think I knew what he meant.

One of the more pleasant memories I have about the college was the cuisine. Inmates from the neighbouring Polmont Young Offenders Institution served the most amazingly presented meals in the staff restaurant, cooked by trained catering officers, helped ably by the under 21 year olds. These young inmates were being trained to City & Guilds level and the quality of their cooking was noteworthy.

The impressive dining room was elaborately decorated with ornate furnishings and formally laid out with fresh, crisp white-linen tablecloths and napkins. On special nights, quality silver centrepieces adorned the tables along with porcelain plates and crystal glasses. This place was far better than most restaurants I had been to in my time. Ok, I was only 22-years old, so probably quite easily pleased, but I do remember being pretty impressed, if not a little intimidated by it all.

Everyone sat at the same 'table for four' each night with the same guys and I have never been so happy to share a table with three cigarette smokers. The young inmates who had served our table each night kept us happy by leaving us extra helpings of food and only because they would be 'tipped' by my mates leaving them a few cigarettes in return, surreptitiously hidden under their napkins for them to find while clearing our table afterwards. I wasn't a smoker but I reaped the benefits by association. No verbal was ever exchanged between my dining companions and the young category 'D' inmates, but they always knew exactly which table to bring all those leftover portions to first!

At that time, every prisoner on admission was given a category. If you were assigned as category D, you were able to work outside the prison unsupervised by staff. Category C prisoners were permitted to work unsupervised inside the perimeter but had to have an officer with them if they worked outside the jail. Category B was the most common of all and they had to be escorted when outside their residential block at all times. Category A inmates were kept under constant surveillance and was reserved for terrorists, persistent escapers and other more extraordinary crimes.

These young waiters of ours were mostly short-term first offenders that were unlikely to be inside for anything worse than not wearing a seatbelt, having no television licence or smoking downstairs on a bus! Okay I *am* exaggerating, but their crimes were mostly petty.

One morning when all of us raw recruits were getting prepared to go into the lecture theatre for that day's culture shock, a call was announced through the intercom system that all twenty-nine of us were to be addressed by the College Principal, a governor grade. Oh dear, it turned out that some envious blabbermouth had got wind of the 'fags for food' scam and had reported it. The Principal hadn't been told who had been accused of such a scandalous act of compassion toward the young inmates, but he let it be known that if he ever did find out who it was they would all be, 'Doon the road faster than shite through a mongoose!'

Our wee feeding frenzy was brought to a halt and we almost faded away to the size of baby hippos during the remainder of the course. Marching on a near-empty stomach felt like we were being held at Tenko and had been cruelly punished.

After being drilled on the parade ground for almost an hour we were taken to the lecture theatre each morning for classes. I found it amusing how they called it a lecture theatre and not a classroom.

"The SPS College welcomes you to its Lecture Theatre, where today's pantomime will include roll play on security, social issues and illegal substances."

On one of the more entertaining mornings in class, we had two police officers from Strathclyde drugs squad who came and gave us a lecture on illegal substances and it was extremely pleasurable.

A 9oz bar of cannabis resin was passed around the recruits along with a Zippo lighter. We were then invited to light the corner of said cannabis and smell its strong pungent aroma. The supposition was that none of us knew what cannabis smelled like, so it could be valuable if we ever came across the odour in the course of our duty. I had smelled it loads of times and will admit now to having had the odd toke or three. Who did the cops think we were, a classroom full of choirboys? This was high quality stuff these officers had brought in and the 9oz bar was being well taken advantage of. The classroom smelled like an Amsterdam Coffee Shop by the time the police finished the lecture and we all left for lunch giggling like a roomful of schoolgirls, happy, high and strangely very hungry!

The prison college housed its very own 'Black Museum', a room heaving with glass cabinets and small display cases, full of items that had been discovered and confiscated from convicts in various prisons through the decades. Home-made slashing tools had been made by melting toothbrush handles and then setting the blades extracted from disposable razors into the softened plastic until they hardened; unsophisticated and simple to make but lethal, brutal and very callous. False passports, homespun ropes, hammers, axes and escape kits had all been collected from foiled breakout attempts throughout the years; homemade keys and various disguise kits were a regular find. One ingenious prisoner had made himself an officer's uniform complete with hat badge, shirt, tie and epaulettes. I remember being shocked that he'd managed to get the detail so accurate. Robbie Conn, whom I was now shadowing at Barlinnie, were on the usual boring backshift in 'A' Hall and him and I got talking to an older officer about the contraband tools which prisoners had allegedly made and he told us,

'That's nothing, if you give some of them a roll of sticky-back plastic and a couple of egg boxes, they'll make you a fuckin' television set!'

That's an obvious exaggeration I thought, but after I had served a few years in the SPS I began to understand what he meant. If some of these guys had put the same effort they had used for nefarious purposes into more positive schemes, they could probably have worked out a solution to climate change. Here is a wee example:

Security, as I am sure you will appreciate, is paramount in a prison and it was drummed into you from day one.

Officers and key-holding civilian staff were not permitted to let prisoners even clap eyes on a key let alone touch one. The reason being that in the past, prisoners had surreptitiously constructed makeshift keys in the metal-fabrication workshops by taking an impression of a key using a bar of soap. Some dopey, unsuspecting screw would be distracted by a couple of cons, humoured and pick-pocketed or naively coerced, his keys would then be swiftly copied using the aforementioned 'soapy' method and put back into his pocket before he could shout, 'Imperial Leather!' You had to have eyes in the back of your head to work in some jails, especially Barlinnie.

All the necessary tools and equipment were at their disposal to carry out most illicit tasks, all they had to do was find a way of distracting the screws while they 'borrowed' them for a wee while. Even some of the methods that they used to smuggle in drugs were impressive.

Barlinnie at that time had around fifteen hundred prisoners and naturally they generated a lot of food waste; therefore seagulls would never be too far away from the open skips outside the prison kitchen even though Barlinnie was about thirty five miles from the nearest beach as the gull flies.

Some 'raptor expert' on the outside would catch and kill a seagull. It would then be gutted and relieved of its innards and its belly packed full of heroin, cocaine, money or anything else that had been ordered from inside the prison. The poor bird was then carefully stitched up and made to look new again, before being taken to the jail when it was dark; most likely by an ex con who was familiar with the layout of where he was going to throw it. I mean, who's going to bat an eyelid at another dead seagull lying amongst the litter and debris?

The inside of the prison was constantly patrolled during the day by one or two old lags who were on what was colloquially termed 'bomb patrol' with their wooden barrow. They would then collect the dead bird, bag it and deliver its contents to the prearranged addressee.

You might be wondering why the term 'bomb patrol' was used? At that time there was no cell sanitation in Barlinnie so rather than defecate in their plastic chamber pot and whiff out their rooms, inmates used to place the offending brown article in a newspaper and throw it out of the cell window.

'Welcome to Barlinnie: Where today's news is tomorrows shit wrapper!'

Willie Ferguson, a colleague and friend of mine, told me he was escorting legendary songsmith and socialist Billy Bragg around the prison when he was in Barlinnie to perform a gig. Willie advised the singers' crew to move their parked van from underneath the windows of 'B' Hall. One of the roadies then laughed and said it was hardly likely to be stolen as they were inside a prison staffed by hundreds of officers. As Willie was trying to explain to him that it wasn't for the fear of the van being nicked that he should move it, when a large, heavy newspaper full of shite struck the roof of the vehicle and splashed on the ground at their feet. The guy immediately stopped laughing and moved the van.

Many denizens of the Bar-L have been hit on the head by a warm 'bomb' as they walked underneath the cellblocks. Fortunately, I managed to avoid being struck by any of these soft sidewinders.

One thing I never managed to avoid though was the smell at the start of an early shift standing in the arch. The arch was the name given to the large toilet area at the end of each landing, so called because of the original stone arch that the prisoners had to walk through to access the old toilet block, these dated facilities were latterly replaced with modern ablutions.

At 6am each morning the staff went round every cell counting each prisoner through their spy-hole, ascertaining they were alive by kicking the door to make sure they were 'moving'. The totals were then passed downstairs to the main desk. Once the totals were calculated and affirmed, the words 'Numbers correct - open them up!' would be heard echoing throughout the hall.

One minute there's nobody around and the next, three or four hundred prisoners are rushing out of their cells with plastic pots full of greenish brown liquid, or whatever else they cared to get rid of. This was then deposited down the large sluice bowl only feet from my nose as I stood guard at the arch. The stench completely overwhelmed me and several times I had to walk away from the area for several minutes as the unbearable vapour caught the back of my throat like fish-fart fumes.

The reason an officer stood there in the first place was to ensure that the inmates didn't smash the ceramic sinks, toilet bowls and cisterns; or attack each other when staff weren't around to witness. 6am in Bar-L wasn't the best time to go for a slash, if you pardon the pun.

I hated working shifts, as I wasn't used to starting at the ungodly hour of 6am or getting home from a backshift until nearly 10pm. I had to try and find a way to resolve this small logistical nightmare, once I was more familiar with the regime and how things worked in Barlinnie.

I frequently saw an officer wearing painter's whites over his uniform being followed by two prisoners in paint-splattered clothing. Bob Ferla was the officer's name, a lovely guy with a great sense of humour. He would always stop to speak to me as a fellow 'brother of the brush' whenever he passed me walking through the jail. I would spot Bob coming a mile away as he always had his 'gruesome twosome' following him, or as he coined the passmen, his two wally dugs!

Bob told me that the estates department, which is responsible for the maintenance of the jail, had officers who were also tradesmen; plumbers, joiners, electricians, decorators etc, and this provided a workparty where prisoners could learn valuable skills. This post offered 9am until 5pm constant day shift for suitably qualified officers as well as every weekend off, it also included a specialist allowance on top of your salary into the bargain.

'Haud me back! I'll have to get myself onto that wee group,' I thought. Why not? Everyone else seemed to be carving out a niche for themselves.

A CASE OF BEER AND AN INJURED DEER

I made further enquiries before submitting an application to the relevant department and a few weeks later I was sent to a semi-open jail, HMP Dungavel near Strathaven, to carry out a 'trade test' to ensure that I was qualified and up to the competence required. If I passed this assessment, I would then be considered for a post as a specialist Estates Officer. I couldn't wait to get away from shift working as well as having more money in my wages, a win/win if ever there was one.

The trade test was a cakewalk, in which I had to strip and repaper the staircase of big Peter Somerville's three-bedroom prison quarter. Peter was a delightful guy; a big ginger-haired, red-faced, freckly fat farmer type who was in charge of the gardens party; a squad of about ten long-term category D prisoners. These men worked outside the prison perimeter cutting grass and pulling weeds, as well as tidying the communal areas that surrounded the staff quarters. These houses were built only a few hundred metres from the gate but were cleverly concealed through the woods just outside the perimeter fence. I got to know all of Peter's outside workers during the four weeks or so that I was stationed there and they were all very friendly and sociable.

Dungavel was more like a small county hospital than a prison. It held long-term adult males who were deemed not to pose a danger to the public. Amongst these men were three LTP's (long term prisoners) nearing the end of their sentences; one was a bent cop who was transferred there to keep him isolated from the mainstream population in other jails for his own safety. I mean police are hated in jail but dishonest ones, exponentially so. A dishonest solicitor who couldn't keep his paws out of his clients' bank accounts was now scraping out weeds between the paths with a small hand tool alongside a lifer who had apparently, 'Found The Lord!'

Why hadn't he had found the Lord *before* he went berserk and murdered his parents? I thought. That would have been real divine intervention. I encountered that kind of thing several times during my service, inmates finding religion. If it helps I suppose, why not? As the John Lennon song goes, 'Whatever gets you through your life!'

Every morning in the estates yard the 'works' staff, as they were known, and their prisoners would have a quick cup of coffee and a discussion before the day ahead. These discussions could be about anything, from tasks that were due to be carried out that day, to the football match on the telly the previous night. It was a friendly place Dungavel and the sort of jail I could have seen myself working in long-term.

Stevie, a prisoner who worked in the gardens workparty was from Stepps, a couple of miles from the village where I lived. We used to sit and blether about guys whom we both knew from our area as we drank our coffee and although he looked familiar, I never knew Stevie on the outside. He told me who in Dungavel to be wary of and pointed out the 'good guys' and the 'wankers' from both sides of the divide. He was hilarious and one of the aforementioned good guys that kept me entertained each morning before the shift began. After my month was up, I was actually sad that I wouldn't be seeing 'Stevie the Counterfeiter' again unless I bumped into him at my local Coop, although I'd probably have to avert my eyes at the till just in case he was passing dodgy banknotes!

A month was actually a generous amount of time that I had been given to carry out my trade test. In reality, if I had taken a month to paper a staircase this size when I worked with Transform, I would have owed the company money. I assumed that the extra time provided was to ensure that you took your time and didn't cut any corners.

Trevor Marshall, the senior officer who inspected and marked my work, was a decorator to trade as well as being a pedantic nerd type who liked the sound of his own voice. He loved working in Dungavel and he would walk to Peter's house with me every morning to update and check on my progress. A wee bit unnecessary I thought, but I had nothing to hide.

I was now well into my third week at Peter's house and I was working alone this particular morning. Peter was at work and his wife had gone out in the car somewhere. It was around 10:30am and I was sweating like the accused in the dock as I steam-stripped the paper from the stairwell walls. My tranquility was shattered when the doorbell rang; it was Stevie from Peter's workparty.

'Sorry to bother you John, but I didn't know what to do with this!' he announces, as he opens his parka-style coat to show the face of a tiny baby deer peeking out.

I tried to speak, "What the f...'

'I found it just lying in the woods out in a clearing. I think it's been attacked by something because it can't walk,' Stevie tells me with a concerned look on his face.

'We'll have to take it back to the gate Stevie, animal rescue would want to take a look at that.' I tell him.

His expression changed from concerned to quiet acceptance as I locked Peter's front door and walked the five hundred or so metres back to the prison gate with Stevie and 'Bambi'. The poor wee thing was visibly shaking under his coat like a washing machine on a high-speed spin cycle.

Stan, the old officer at the gate came out to greet us in the usual manner. Dungavel didn't have an enclosed gatelodge like a secure prison. Instead, the gate officer came out of a sentry-style shed next to the main building to manually open a large pair of mesh vehicle gates. These were set into the single perimeter fence with a smaller, 7-foot by 3-foot pedestrian aperture (Judas gate) built into it.

'You're back early Stevie!' Stan said to the inmate, 'What have you got there?'

'He found an injured baby deer!' I answer.

The gate officer looks confused so Stevie opens his parka once again to reveal a tiny black nose attached to the cutest wee face I've ever seen. The fawn peeks out at the old screw, bewildered.

'OOH, a deer?' the screw said, as he eventually recognizes the mammal. 'A female deer!' Stevie answers facetiously, before adding,

'We left Ray and a drop of golden sun in the woods!' Stevie winked at me before whistling the song from 'A Sound of Music'. The old screw looked puzzled as he drew us a baffled look. I don't think he was the sharpest knife in the toolbox, even though his name was Stanley!

Thankfully, Peter Somerville was delighted with his staircase and on my last day at Dungavel he handed me a case of beer as I got into my car in the car park, nice one. It was a real pleasurable experience working at such a prison, which was unlike any other jail I have worked in since.

The following week, word came through to Barlinnie that I had passed my trade test, even though Trevor Marshall had tried to intimidate me by shadowing me like a reflection every morning. That didn't matter, as I was now being offered a golden opportunity and my mission was to transfer to Glenochil should I chose to accept it. It took me all of 2 seconds to make that decision. I told 'her indoors' that my transfer was compulsory as it made more sense than telling her that I had a choice, even if it was only *take it or leave it.* I wanted away from Barlinnie so much that I'd have taken a transfer to one of the Russian Gulag Archipelagos had that been on offer!

Incidentally, to the UK's shame, Dungavel was converted and sadly now used as an immigration detention centre where entire families; women, children and the elderly are kept incarcerated, some of them for years.

The time elapsed from passing my trade test to then being transferred seemed to pass slower than a turtle with a bad limp and I seemed to be constantly checking with George at the transfer desk for updates. Eventually the director's order came through and I was to be moved at public expense to HMP Glenochil as soon as the transfer could be enacted.

A transfer at public expense was certainly a lucrative deal and being funded by the government meant that you had all of your relocation expenses reimbursed such as estate agent and solicitors fees, furniture removal costs and five days special leave to look at houses. I wasn't out of pocket by even a single penny as everything was paid for and I was recompensed for the fuel that I used looking for aforementioned houses. When I say everything was paid for I mean everything, even to the extent of having central heating fitted if the new home didn't have it, as well as a new television aerial and the refitting of your washing machine at the new house too. Officers being moved under these circumstances could also claim up to half of their annual salary as a lump-sum interest-free loan, and could suspend the repayments of such for up to two years. I would happily have accepted a transfer every year as long as these financial arrangements were in place.

Unfortunately this was the only occasion that I was ever moved at public expense, as my subsequent transfer eight years later was only seven miles and a ten-minute drive away.

Glenochil was only around thirty miles from Barlinnie but in terms of aesthetics and pastoral splendour it was a million miles from the Glasgow area and I welcomed the change of lifestyle with anticipation and excitement.

One of the first things that I noticed about living in the Glenochil area was my car and home insurance premiums. They were almost half the cost of what they had been in Glasgow. The tempo that life seemed to move at here was so unhurried that it took me a while to appreciate it. The roads seemed much quieter too and my stress levels had reduced considerably, due to there not being enough fellow drivers on the rural roads for me to rage at; even the bars and restaurants seemed quieter and more carefree. I had made the right decision to move here.

The house that I bought was a typical three-bedroom semi, the type shown at that time on television drama series Brookside; red brick cuboids of various sizes and configurations all facing inwards toward the cul-de-sac. I had arrived in middle-class suburbia, it was February 1987 and the start of the next chapter in my position as a 'Soldier of the State'.

GALLAGHER'S SALUTE AND THE LIGHTS WENT OOT!

Thinking back to my first few days as a screw, I had always found it astonishing that a lot of prisoners seemed to be just wandering around inside the perimeter walls. I remember thinking that at any time they wanted, these guys could have easily taken over the place. I soon learnt that *that* was indeed the case; a prison only runs efficiently by the cooperation of its inmates.

This became manifestly clear on 5th January 1987 when a hall full of officers were taken hostage, some of them dragged onto the roof at knifepoint and threatened with being thrown off. The subsequent riot that ensued cost the treasury millions and was the longest running Scottish prison siege in history. Inmates, who had managed to break out onto the roof, threw slates at prison staff. Prisoners who took over large areas of the jail dropped large stone blocks on officers in riot gear. Then, alleging they had been the victims of brutality took five staff hostage and started fires, setting fire to cell doors with prisoners and officers inside. Their screams for help could be heard outside in the staff quarters.

Two of the hostages were released but the rest were held as masked convicts claimed the attic space and roof, hurling abuse at the then governor, Andrew Gallagher. They paraded their hostages dressed in prisoners' clothing onto the prison roof in front of the worlds press like macabre trophies. Bed sheets were adorned with various accusatory slogans scrawled on them and wrapped around the prison's massive chimney stacks.

'SLASHER GALLAGHER IS BRUTALITY' one banner read.

He had apparently earned the nickname Slasher when he worked in Peterhead jail in the 70's. It was rumoured that he drew a knife across a prisoner's face after the con had lunged at him and allegedly tried to stick the small blade into the Governor's neck first. The bold Gallagher had supposedly taken the knife from him and stuck it into the cons face. The incident had been hushed up and Gallagher was later transferred elsewhere, a favourite ploy in the SPS at the time. I only met the man a few times and I thought that he was a complete megalomaniac. He would make every officer salute him as they passed each morning, while he waved at them like a fat Adolf Hitler in his pork-pie hat and woollen trench coat!

I remember Gallagher walking through the hall one morning on his rounds when I overheard a prisoner say to his pal,

'I wouldn't be surprised if one mornin' he walked through here with swastikas sewn onto that fuckin' coat!'

He certainly had that mad dictator look about him right enough, but I couldn't ascertain if the slashing incident was true.

I had been fortunate enough to be working in a different hall when the riot kicked off in 'B' Hall. Alarm bells seemed to be ringing constantly and about ten of us were ordered into the offending hall. I was met with a scene of complete devastation and utter chaos. Metal beds, mattresses, chairs, pipes, concrete blocks and wardrobes still full of clothes were being thrown off the galleries and landing with the force of a mini explosion right in front of us. Fires were glowing in every corner you looked and extinguishers were either being used legitimately or thrown like missiles from above. Orders were being barked out and inmates were shouting obscenities and throwing whatever they could find at every screw they saw. The whole place was in tatters.

Less than a month earlier I had been issued with a directors order to be transferred to Glenochil Prison near Alloa and it couldn't come quick enough! Meanwhile, I had to ride this tsunami of sewage until then.

The place had been buzzing for weeks and inmates were getting restless with fights being a regular occurrence. I remember one shift when an inmate had been set alight in 'B' Hall exercise yard. This happened regularly. The target would be furtively sprayed with lighter fluid from a small tin as he walked past and then another prisoner walking from the opposite direction would throw a match at him, and up he went like a roman candle. Unknown to me, the whole jail was about to blow. The word overly used by the media to describe this situation was, a powderkeg! I was hoping that if it did go tits up, I'd be long gone.

Fortunately I played little part in the hostage situation, but dealing with prisoners in the aftermath of the riot that were locked up for 24 hours a day was exhausting both physically and mentally. According to prison rules a prisoner is allowed an hour out of cell exercise each day, but that was soon forgotten about as management wouldn't risk letting anyone else out for fear of it all kicking off again, so the place was in a total lockdown situation for weeks if not months, I really don't know as I managed to get away before I found out that timescale.

This would be unbearable for some inmates who ironically couldn't handle being locked up in their 'Peter' all day. (A Peter is prison slang for a cell.) They would get themselves so wound up that when an officer eventually opened up their cell door he would be drenched in urine, thrown by the angry thug who had been screaming through the gap in his door all day to get out; forcing him to urinate, and occasionally defecate into a plastic chamber pot. Not a great start to your shift especially if you happened to have your mouth open when opening the aforementioned cell door. At least you had the indulgence of a half hours' respite from it all as you went to the staff-rooms to have a shower and change your uniform. This luckily never happened to me.

I say luckily because in general, I feel that I was pretty fortunate when I think back on my time spent inside; more than eighteen years in total if you don't count the time I spent on sick leave suffering from stress. Eighteen years just sounds like a sentence, but it could have been a lot worse. I know guys who were assaulted on a regular basis but I was never physically harmed. I don't know why. I can only assume that it was luck, or maybe it was my laid back approach, I'm not really sure? I tend to treat people the same way they treat me, so if someone is respectful and courteous to me they get that back tenfold. I think inmates maybe cottoned onto this character trait of mine pretty early on in the proceedings and could sense that I was a straight up guy?

If they requested something and it was at my discretion as to whether or not they got it, then as long as they hadn't made a habit of speaking to me like I was something that they'd just scraped off the sole of their shoe, then I made sure that they got what they had requested, and a wee bit more if I felt that their suffering had warranted it. I'm not saying that I was a softy like Mr Barraclough from the BBC TV sitcom *Porridge* or anything like that, but I certainly wasn't the Mr MacKay type either. This became apparent to me one cold, dark November evening. I had been escorting twenty prisoners at a time over to the canteen block where they went every Friday night to sign for their weekly wages and spend it on tobacco, toiletries and sweet treats, etc. The canteen was situated in a dining hall and was about 50 yards from the residential Hall. It was an old prefab style single-storey concrete structure with steel windows and looked like something you would find in an old RAF base during the war.

The third batch of guys were all lined up waiting to be served at the hatch and I was standing at the end of the queue near the door about 20 feet from the serving counter. It was around 8pm when suddenly everything went dark and I heard the metal shutters being pulled down on the kiosk window. The officer inside the booth was concerned for his stock after all the prison lights suddenly went out after the emergency generator had failed during a power cut. There I was left standing in the pitch darkness on my own with twenty raving mad angry convicts who could potentially be a huge security risk as well as being a possible threat to my life; I was in a sticky situation. In fact, I felt I was in a stickier situation than Sticky the stick insect when he got stuck on a sticky bun!

'Right guys settle down!' I shouted in my most convincing voice of authority.

I couldn't see two feet in front of me and I half expected to be jumped on and battered to death at any minute. I thought a pre-emptive strike was the best course of action, so I roared,

'There's obviously been a power cut so nobody's getting served right now. We are all going back to the Hall to wait for the power to be restored.' Without making them aware that I was actually terrified!

A few of them made threats that they weren't going anywhere until they got their tobacco. All I could hear from out of the darkness was,

'You'll be gaun yersel, ya cunt!'

'Fuck off, we're gaun nowhere!'

'That'll be fuckin' right, I've no had ma canteen yet!'

I laughed loudly to try and convince them that I considered their statements as mere Glasgow banter as I opened the exterior door of the canteen to let the small glint of available moonlight seep in through the open door.

'Right guys let's go!' I bawled, and then waited on their response.

Out of the dark I heard a low, threatening voice coming from the crowd of madmen,

'You cunts will dae whit yer telt, he's awrite that big screw!'

Wow! Crooky you are one lucky rookie tonight, I thought.

A con with obvious clout had diffused the situation with one well-timed assertion. I can only assume that he might have been a grateful beneficiary of my altruism at an earlier juncture!

HARRY'S GAGS & MY UNCLES FAGS

My first Barlinnie night shift came along and it was the creepiest of experiences. Hammer Horror hadn't a patch on this place, and to a film producer it would've been an invaluable asset as a location.

At that time there were around 1600 inmates in Barlinnie and once they were all locked securely behind their cell doors, the place got very eerily quiet, except for the odd maniacal scream. The unfamiliar sounds and the way they echoed around the ancient stone buildings, reminded me of the movie Midnight Express. An Alan Parker film from 1978 where an American guy gets thirty years in a brutal Turkish prison for smuggling hash and is subsequently locked up alongside the criminally insane.

All of the main lights in each hall were turned off with only a very dim nightlight being kept on; it was so gloomy you couldn't even see your knees as they trembled. The junior man, i.e. me, was designated C&D patrolman; basically responsible for C Hall and D Hall and making all the compulsory foot patrols as deemed necessary by the

Principal Officer (PO) in charge of the night shift. Your first task as C&D patrolman was to go around every cell door pushing on them to ensure they were securely locked and then putting out each light. I'd heard the story of an officer who nearly landed on a prisoner's bed when pushing on his door while on C&D night patrol, this was because some not so sharp officer hadn't locked the cell door properly when leaving from the back shift!

Sometimes if a prisoner was reading he would ask for his cell light to be left on, so you normally left it until the next time you were passing. When you told him it could be hours later he'd reply, 'That's ok boss, I can sleep all night with a light on.' Prisoners call officers 'boss' when addressing them. It's used as a sort of moniker and can often be heard being used in old American prison movies. The men would sometimes call out to you through their cell door as you passed to ask you something or even just for someone to talk to. I remember one of the guys on my own landing, Harry. He was the gate passman if you recall my meeting him on my first day? I'd left his light on for him as usual and as I passed his door I heard him calling out to me,

'Here boss?'   'Aye?'   'Is that you Crooky?'
'Aye, what is it Harry?'

'What's the difference between light and hard?'

'I don't know Harry, what *is* the difference?'

'You can get to sleep with a light on!' he answered.

'Aye very funny, goodnight Harry!'

He was always telling mad stories, cracking jokes and generally acting the goat. I suppose it was Harry's way of doing his time the easiest way he could. He'd ask me random stuff like,

'Here, boss. Can you drive?'

'Aye, of course I can drive.' I would answer, like the prize numpty I was.

'Well reverse yer arse onto this then!' he would shout, grabbing his crotch and laughing like a drain. He wasn't happy unless he was ripping into someone. I would then chase him like I was going to attack him and Harry would be shouting stuff at me like, 'Take yer hat aff ya big Nancy and we'll have a square go!' Then as I was taking off my hat, he would shout, 'Second thoughts, just keep it on and I'll punch you oot it!' Brilliant!

Harry was now my passman on the 3rd flat of 'A' Hall and he'd stand and drink his tea at the desk with us as he told joke after joke. Most of his jokes weren't really jokes in the true sense of the word. He would just come out with stuff like, 'Hey John, do you like fruit?' 'What kind of question is that Harry? Of course I like fruit!' I would answer, with the water streaming down the back of my ears in a whippersnapper like manner. 'Well suck on *this*, it's a peach!' he'd say, grabbing himself once more as he ran off doubled up with laughter. I'd fall for it every time, he was the sort of slapstick clown who played it straight then slapped you on the kisser with a punchline.

Meanwhile back on the night shift I was doing the usual patrols. I hated it when my route took me through D Hall, as that was where the gallows were located; and although the death penalty in the UK was abolished in 1965, the apparatus for carrying out the act was still there. I never saw the actual killing device but long-serving staff would often bring up the subject when I had spent the occasional overtime shift working alongside them in D Hall.

The condemned man's room was a double-sized cell and had been continuously in use by four of Barlinnie's current customers. I often wondered what some of their reactions might have been had they known which cell they were occupying?

There was a wooden walkway or bridge, which connected the death cell to the gallows on the opposite side of the landing. Whenever I made my night shift route past those doors, I often thought about the condemned men who had made that short walk before me. I crept quietly past the doors that led to the gallows, the very ones that they had walked through on their last short stride to the knotted rope. The walk past those doors would be made doubly eerie by the fact that the floor here was still made of wooden floorboards and they echoed your footsteps around the hall a lot louder than the other areas. I don't know why this section remained in wood; every other floor in the Hall had been converted to solid concrete.

Historically, all executions were traditionally carried out at 8am and as their bodies were legally the property of the state, the deceased were buried in unmarked graves within the perimeter walls of the jail. Years later the remains of all the executed prisoners were subsequently exhumed and reburied elsewhere. I remember an old screw that had worked at Barlinnie for 30 years told me a week after I had started in the place that Peter Manuel, a notorious murderer, was buried under a large flagstone close to the door of D Hall.

That hall had always given me the creeps and there were stories circulating around the jail that an officer whom I had known as big Stretch, had refused to work in D Hall ever again after seeing a misty fog coming from under the gallows door and a shadowy figure appearing through the mist on his night shift. My logical side told me that there had to be a reasonable explanation for this 'phenomena'. I thought someone must have left a shower running and he had seen his own reflection in a pane of glass or something, or that possibly the outside patrol staff were boiling a kettle behind the door to wind him up, but if the officer believes what he saw and is 100% adamant, then who was I not to believe him? I'm not surprised he was terrified. I was telling big Stretch and I mentioned that it was, '…enough to give you the willies.' He said, 'I bet plenty of guys have been given the willies in D Hall!'

There were lighter moments in Barlinnie too. The jail had its very own chapel, which doubled as a cinema/concert hall. This old building was situated between 'B' Hall and 'C' Hall and was indeed an actual church building; it had a large bell, a steeple, wooden pews the lot. I shouldn't have been surprised really, because a church is needed *more* in a place so full of sinners than anywhere else ... and that's only among the staff!

Tuesday night was 'A' Hall's night for the pictures and I can remember watching the first Terminator movie with three hundred of Scotland's finest and 'Movie Night' in the Bar-L chapel was the funniest picture house in Glasgow, bar none. Eight officers sat on bespoke high chairs down each side of the chapel. The chairs were so high that your head was nearly eight feet from the ground and with the prisoners all seated on normal chairs this meant we had an excellent view of them and the screen.

All you could hear were random yells of, 'WHIT'S THIS PISH?' 'THIS IS PURE MINCE!' 'SHITE!'

Pay attention Mr Spielberg, these were the kind of reviews you got from the patrons of the Bar-L if your movie wasn't up to their usual lofty standards!

'Some'dy shoot that fuckin' projectionist!' and 'Lock me up boss, ah cannae handle this anymair!' were typical critique's of what we heard occasionally being yelled out from the sea of heads that were laid out below us. Nobody actually cared who said it and I just found it really comical when they behaved in this way.

Watching the film perched up high on the elevated stools was very uncomfortable as there were no horizontal bars running along at foot level to rest your feet on. Therefore your legs were just left dangling like two ham ends in a butchers window. There had been foot supports on the chairs at one time but they had to be removed years previously when more than one complacent officer had got themselves very comfy and settled in to watch the movie and had then fallen asleep.

The final straw came when one officer tumbled off the high-stool like the cannonball in 'Indiana Jones' and rolled down on top of the prisoners sat underneath him; a Temple of Doom right enough. He scattered them like skittles and broke his ankle in the process. The Governor was told that the staff were using the opportunity to settle in and watch a movie instead of observing the cons, so his solution to the problem was to have the foot support bars sawn off the stools!

Clever? Or just a cop out? You decide.

I once had the pleasure of my uncle's company when he was remanded for a week or two. I was standing in the corner of 'C' Hall exercise yard watching the throng of inmates wandering around me in the usual massive circle, when out of the gloom I recognised a familiar face. It was Eddie, my dad's younger brother; he would have been around thirty-five at the time. I cornered him when there was nobody around and asked him what had happened and how he had managed to get himself locked up in this hellhole? He told me that he'd been remanded for social enquiry reports following a bar brawl in a Coatbridge pub, nothing serious he said. I asked him if any of the family knew he was inside, he said that nobody knew. 'Do you want me to contact anyone for you Eddie?' I asked, concerned for my uncle's welfare.

'I suppose you could tell your dad', he answered.

I really don't know what, if anything, he expected my dad to do. But when I told my dad I'd met my uncle Eddie in the Bar-L that day, let's just say he wasn't rushing up to visit him! I tried to reassure him that we are not our brother's keeper; meaning he wasn't responsible for Eddie's actions and that anyone can end up in jail for lots of reasons. I think he just felt a bit embarrassed about it all. Fortunately, Eddie wasn't on the same landing as me. His cell was on the floor below, so I bought him 20 Embassy Regal from the prison canteen and proceeded downstairs. As I scoured the large melamine board on the second floor for his name to check what cell he was in, Ronnie, the officer in charge of that landing, approached me.

'Who are you looking for?' he asked me. 'Crook' I answered reluctantly.

'Is that Eddie Crook? He's in number five John.' he giggled and then enquired frivolously, 'Is he yer faither??'

'Aye Ronnie, we're going to have a big tearful reunion in cell number five!' I glare jokingly at him, and then laughed as I walked along the narrow walkway to unlock my uncle Eddie's cell. If only Ronnie knew how close he was to the truth.

'Crook?' I asked, looking in turn at the two guys lying on their single metal-framed beds. I must admit that the irony of opening a cell door and asking which one of the two prisoners was a Crook was lost on me at the time.

'That's me boss.' Eddie answered innocently, so as not to arouse the suspicion of his oblivious cellmate that we were in fact related.

'1-2-3 O'Leary, asked me to drop these into you.' I lied for the same reason, before lobbing the 20 smokes in his direction.

'Thanks son!' he answered, almost blowing our cover.

I never saw Eddie in his stripey shirt again as I was subsequently transferred as directed, but Glenochil brought fresh new challenges, and very different ones, which I will document in later chapters.

Although I was now assigned a post in 'C' Hall, Barlinnie's 'A' Hall was my first appointed area to work. I had started my career on the second flat with an experienced officer of 12 years, a lovely fella named Robbie Conn. Which was highly amusing for both staff as well as inmates, given that my surname is Crook, you can fill in a lot of the jokes here yourself.

Each landing had 55 cells and all of them were occupied, most of them with 2 occupants. The prison rules stated that officers were not supposed to let out any more prisoners than he or she could physically handle. I mean, the more I actually thought about it most officers, myself included, could hardly handle *one* at a time never mind a number of them. This directive was just a safeguarding mechanism for management so that they could beat you over the head with the rulebook if something went wrong. If every officer worked to that rule, absolutely nothing would ever get done.

According to those same regulations, if the number of prisoners being held on a landing went over 70 because of new admissions, transfers etc., then control would send us a third man as a 'security' officer. They sent an old screw by the name of Jimmy Hood over to us for an overtime shift one night near Christmas and that evening's pantomime was well under way starring Hood, Conn and Crook. I think we had nearly a hundred inmates on our flat that night. Wee Harry our passman was in his element.

'You couldnae make this shit up, John!' he said.

Harry and I would call each other by our first names if there were no one else within earshot; it was a kind of mutual respect thing. Robbie Conn and Jimmy Hood were standing beside me at the small desk at the top of the stairs when Harry arrives, pointing at the three of us as he taunts, 'Hood, Conn and Crook! The Three Wise Monkeys – Hear Evil, See Evil and Do Evil!' We all laughed and Harry and his two pals were laughing that much they had sore ribs at the end of the shift. I had prisoners, who had never spoken a word to me previously, come up and ask,

'Boss, your name's no' Crook is it? That's fuckin' brilliant!'

It seemed to release a lot of tension and the backshift went really quickly. Harry sniggered as I locked his cell door for the night and left his light on for him as usual. He shouted from behind his locked cell door to me, as I walked away,

'Crooky?'

'Aye, what is it Harry?'

'I've never laughed so much since my granny got her tits caught in the mangle!'

BIG FAT SCREWS & ILLICIT BOOZE

Strategically placed all around Barlinnie, and every other prison for that matter, were alarm bell points. If staff needed assistance for whatever reason, inmates fighting usually, they would press these alarm buttons, and officers of all shapes and sizes would appear from all over the jail, as if by magic.

Some of these guys were heavy-duty screws built like the proverbial 'brick shithouse'. They could barely walk, let alone run. Their thighs were so fat that they rubbed together whenever they tried to run and a few of them almost spontaneously combusted in the trouser region with the friction! 'Chub Rub' I believe it's called nowadays.

God alone knows what they would've been like if they'd encountered a serious incident when they arrived at the scene and found themselves 'rag-dolled' on the floor with a bunch of angry cons? Some of them would've needed oxygen and a bed bath after their 200-yard dash to provide 'assistance'. Wee Harry would say to us,

'Here boss, that fat useless lump o' wid would be no use for anything as long as he had a hole in his arse!'

It was not long after I started in the SPS that they introduced fitness testing for all prison officers. Not before time, I thought. Some of these fat boys were so big they made Jabba The Hutt look like Kate Moss. Their uniform shirts and trousers had to be specially made for them. The shirts were like duvet covers and the trousers had to have large triangular sections sewn into the seat.

Prisoners at Perth jail made staff uniforms at that time, and I can imagine their laughter when they saw the size of the garments they had to stitch together. Occasionally a member of staff would complain that their new trousers were making them itch; on further inspection it was found that the mischievous machinists from the textile workshop in Perth, who had evidently carried out their own unique brand of quality control, had sewn a layer of steel wool into the crotch just to provide that wee bit of extra comfort! Ouch!

The laundry in Barlinnie was run by one of those aforementioned 'heavy- duty screws'. Derek would be responsible for all the prisoners' clothing in the jail, including towels and suchlike. If Derek's kit-store passmen were short of any of this apparel, he would make it his business to have a tour around all the halls screaming up like a mental case at the screws to send down any spare kit that they could gather. I remember the first time I witnessed him doing this; I asked the officer I was working with, 'Who is that big guy?'

'That's the Night Rider!' he answers with a sardonic smile. 'The Night Rider?' I enquired, looking puzzled.

'Aye, David Hasselhoff??' He says and with a broad grin appearing on his face, adds, 'It's because he's always looking for KIT!'

It was the eighties and I don't expect everyone to catch that obscure reference, so for those that don't; KIT was the name of the robot car in the 1980's TV show *Night Rider* and Hasselhoff's character was continually trying to locate it.

Kind of wastes it when the joke needs explaining though doesn't it? Therefore, if you find any other random, obscure or incomprehensible anecdotes as you read this, it may be wiser to research them yourself should you need further clarification and/or explanation!

These kit searches provided a great excuse for officers to have a rummage around in guys' cells as they then had a legitimate reason to be snooping around; and all sorts of contraband would subsequently be found, from wee bits of hash to gallons of homemade booze or 'hooch' as it was referred to. The inmates would ferment it and hide it in 5 litre plastic containers that were normally used to contain floor cleaning chemicals or polish etc. They would then tape one or two of them to each side of a brush shaft and make out that these 'disinfectant' containers were now being used as weights for a workout and were only filled with water. Quite ingenuous.

If the hooch was found, the officers would stab holes into the bottom of the containers allowing the liquid to spill out all over the tiled floor, then order the prisoner to clean up the mess. If I had been the prisoner and the hooch was mine, I can imagine it would've been slurped off the floor!

BLEEDING IN AN ALLEY IN DOG SHIT VALLEY

Barlinnie was fringed outside its perimeter walls by staff housing known as 'the quarters', which were colloquially referred to by some as 'Dog Shit Valley'. There are always plenty of tales concerning residents in most Glasgow housing schemes and Barlinnie Quarters were no different; sex, violence and shady deals were the default position.

The quarters were mostly laid out to six-in-a-block flats and terraced villas with the occasional semi-detached house and one or two detached, which historically were occupied by governors before Maggie Thatcher's *right to buy* policy had sold them off at a fraction of their value.

I had heard the hushed jokes and sexual innuendos that crackled around the jail like wildfire regarding an OMO soap powder box that had frequently appeared in an officer's kitchen window.

'What does that mean, Robbie?' I asked my colleague. 'OMO?', said Robbie with a grin.

'Yea, that guy said somebody's wife used to put an OMO box in her kitchen window and they were all laughing, what's that all about?' I asked him.

Robbie smiled and then told me that OMO wasn't only a washing powder brand, it was an acronym and it meant 'On My Own.' Apparently, she used to put the box on the windowsill when her husband went out to work to let her bit(s) on the side know that she was now alone!

Around December 1985 in the very same staff quarters, I heard about an unfortunately dark incident that occurred in the wee small hours of the morning. I felt a real unease about this when I was told the story straight from the donkey's mouth.

Big Stevie, a screw, was lying in his bed at around 2am when he heard someone stomping around in his ground floor flat, so he got up to investigate. On opening the door to the kitchen he was confronted by the sight of a housebreaker.

'I mean, who the fuck has the cheek to break into a prison quarter?' he asked me, rhetorically.

He then told me how he launched himself at the guy, put him in a classic headlock and proceeded to 'beat seven different colours of shite out of him!'

He then dragged the haplessly unfortunate burglar out into the alley where he dumped him unceremoniously into the gutter, bleeding and almost unconscious. He then calmly walked back inside, picked up the phone and called the police to complain that some drunk was causing a disturbance at the back of his house!

Stevie reckoned that the guy wasn't about to tell the cops a screw beat him up, as he would have been incriminating himself in the housebreaking. I asked him what happened to the fella.

'The cops arrived and arrested the cunt for a breach of the peace!' he answered, heehawing with laughter.

'Holy Christ! What sort of a maniac was I working with here?' I thought.

Sitting right in the middle of those staff houses was the Barlinnie Officers Club, or 'THE BOC', as it was affectionately known. At that time it was housed in an old tenement building with bricked up windows, stone floors and bare walls. It looked like one of the roughest and most violent pubs in Glasgow, even ex-cons would think twice about going into this bear pit. I was in the place only the once, even if it was just to say I had been there. Ironically enough, the local pub outside Barlinnie was named The Anvil. We used to joke that this was because in olden times the cons went there to have their ball and chain removed!

I told Robbie Conn that I'd been in the BOC for a pint on the way home one night and he laughed and said,

'Aye you're quite right mate, I'd try anything once,' before adding, 'Except a cock up my arse!'

They used to hold stripper nights in the BOC every so often, and the committee sold tickets at the gatelodge to officers coming off the back shift, so inappropriate when I look back now. But hey it was the eighties, and like a lot of other things, it was acceptable in the eighties!

Stories would surface in the jail the following morning about how the stripper had 'wee Tam' tied to a chair the previous night dressed only in his boxers, stuffing her smalls into his mouth and sitting on his knee totally starkers. She teased him by shoving her breasts in his face before whipping off his boxers to reveal his Chihuahua-sized chipolata.

Tam loved it, even though there were around a hundred or so of his workmates bawling at him and laughing in the shadows, Tam felt like he was *The Man,* it was his moment and he was going to enjoy it!

It's amazing what passes for entertainment with some of these Neanderthal types!

I had been rostered to work on the 3rd flat of 'C' Hall on an early shift. The usual boring routine stuff had occurred between 6am and lunchtime. After lunch the standard shout of, 'Open up for exercise: OUTSIDE!' was heard echoing around the vast reverberating hall. This was the gaffer downstairs on the bottom flat letting all his staff know that he wanted the inmates to be let outside into the exercise yard. This I began doing and by the time I got about a quarter of the way around, my co-worker, Ronnie Mackay, said he was going outside with the prisoners as was the normal practice and I carried on opening the rest of the cells.

Once I was certain they'd all gone outside, I locked all the cells and proceeded to join Ronnie and the rest of the staff, along with two or three hundred remand inmates, in the exercise yard.

I made my way downstairs and was walking in the direction of the short corridor leading out into the yard when a few inmates were walking back into the hall towards me.

"Where are you all going?" I asked them.

"We've to come back in boss, somebody's climbed onto the roof!" was their answer.

It turned out that one of the prisoners I had let out only a few minutes earlier, had ran straight outside and climbed up a drainpipe and onto the roof of the prison. He was protesting that he had been wrongly remanded and had been 'fitted up by the polis' for something that he hadn't done! He had planned it well; he even had a T-shirt with a slogan scrawled on it, he knew the press would turn up and was ready for them with his protest kit.

'FITTED UP - I AM INNOCENT' or words to that effect.

It was quite a plucky act on his part, as those roofs are perilously slippy and at least fifty feet high. Not somewhere you would climb onto if you weren't serious about your protest. He appeared to believe he had a genuine grievance and most likely he had.

Later on that day a few of us were offered a night shift on overtime as we technically had a potential escaper on our hands with Sammo being sat on the roof like he was. I agreed to do it, as it was easy money at the enhanced rate. I hadn't realised though, that I would be standing outside freezing my arse off all night, as the guy hadn't come down yet and had in fact stayed out on the roof until the early hours, only agreeing to go back to his cell when my shift was about to end!

A SHED DOOR WITH BLOOD ON THE FLOOR!

Another cold dark winter Monday morning in the staff muster room and I had been rostered to work a shift on a shed door. This meant I was responsible for keeping a tally of the number of inmates in a workshop. If a member of staff was taking any prisoners away for visits, doctor appointments, social work etc., then the doorman adjusts the workparty numbers and carries out a quick rub down search to ensure no weapons, tools or contraband were being concealed.

At the end of each morning or afternoon session, any tools that were being used are handed into the workshop instructor who then places them on the shadow board. This is a large white board with the shape of every tool in the workshop painted onto it in black. A wee nail is hammered in at the top of each 'shadow' to hang the tool from. This ensures that a tool check can be carried out quickly and efficiently.

Once the instructors are happy that everything is accounted for, the next task was to carry out a rub down search of every prisoner in the workparty as they left. Usually there were extra officers drafted in to help with this, as there could be as much as a hundred or so in each party.

'Awrite John, how are you doing mate?' says the prisoner that I'm searching.

I glanced up quickly to look at his face, as I wasn't paying attention to any individual persons; I was on autopilot as usual. It was Hamish Crawford, a guy whom I had known for years and lived in the next village to mine. Hamish had been in my local pub the previous weekend and was, at one point in the evening, even sitting at our table with his pint.

'Hiya Hamish!' I answered with surprise, continuing my rub down search of him like this was the way we usually met.

'What's happened?' I asked, puzzled.

Before he had time to tell me his story, he'd been swept along with the rest of the fast-moving route as he shouted a series of incoherent words to me like drugs, polis, lifted, two months. I never saw him again after that, and several months later rumours had started to circulate around our local area that Hamish was found under a bridge. He had died of a heroin overdose with the needle still sticking in his arm.

I was working an extra shift in the remand block one evening and a new admission had been sent upstairs to my 3rd flat landing. I got chatting to the guy, named Rory, who said he'd been downstairs on the bottom flat (ground floor) for a few nights having been placed on Capital Charge Observation. It is the job of the bottom flat staff to keep a close watch on C.C.O's just in case they decide that life isn't worth living and they'd prefer to end it all. Rory decided he'd rather live and told me he was confident that he would be found not guilty.

To cut to the chase here, it transpired that he had coincidentally been with Hamish on the night they were both taking heroin and because Hamish never had the ability to pierce his skin with a needle, he had asked Rory to administer the muddy looking grime for him. Rory duly obliged and the rest of his story established for me the accuracy of the rumours circulating around our local area.

Rory was arrested and charged with murder, reduced to culpable homicide by his solicitor. I am not aware of the court's disposal as Rory was on remand for his full statutory 110 days, during which time I was transferred out to Glenochil Young Offenders Institution.

Anyway, back to the shed door, remember?

My afternoon shift in the workshop got underway; this particular workparty was the concrete shop and they made heavy duty building goods such as kerbstones and paving slabs etc., I had locked the door behind me and was just saying a few words to wee Ronnie Macaulay, who was one of the raw recruits that had started the job on the same day as me almost two years previously. We both heard a loud metallic 'CLANG!' and looked over to see one prisoner with a shovel held in both hands and another prisoner stumbling around in a daze. We didn't have to be Miss Marple to speculate what had happened so we both ran toward the pair; but not before the assailant had wrapped the shovel around the other dudes head several more times. In fact the victim's head had more hits than The Beatles and the stone floor was now a lovely bright shade of vermillion.

The governor called in the police and both Ronnie and myself were each precognosed by Strathclyde police detectives. The case being deemed so severe that it went to Glasgow Sheriff Court on a summary procedure. I felt sick at the thought of having to go to court and give my evidence, but it was my job and the citation fell through my letterbox several weeks later.

The courtroom was packed that warm summer morning as I entered the witness box to give my evidence. I had been dreading this moment for months and I felt like everyone would be able to guess that this was my first time in a courtroom. I'd only ever seen them on TV and the whole court process was fascinating to me. My eyes were darting all over the place, as it was all very novel to me. I could see the accused in my peripheral vision sitting in the dock flanked by two prison officers and he was attempting to eyeball me; I assumed he was trying to psych me out and intimidate me, fat chance! Once the clerk of the court affirmed my name and position, the procurator fiscal who had spoken to me earlier, stood up and looked across the courtroom at me,

'Please repeat after his Lordship, Officer Crook,' he says.

An old octogenarian with an antiquated pantomime costume and grey curly horsehair toupee looks over at me and starts to express the oath; I repeat his words verbatim but without his public school accent:

'I solemnly, sincerely and truly declare that I will tell the truth, the whole truth and nothing but the truth.' Says me, with my fingers crossed behind my back for good measure. As I stand in the witness box the procurator fiscal rises to his feet once more and leads me through my statement, which I had provided to the police when they were called to Barlinnie on the afternoon of the offence.

He continues, 'Officer Crook, you say that the accused Mr Campbell, raised a shovel above his head and assaulted the complainer, Mr Stevenson, over the head with it? Can you demonstrate to his Lordship exactly how this occurred?'

I felt awkward standing there while everyone was staring at me, waiting for my feeble amateur dramatic re-enactment of the crime. I know it was necessary to demonstrate to the court exactly what had happened on the day, but there are only so many ways you can lamp someone around the head with a shovel, surely?

I brought my hands together in a clenching motion, raised them above my head and then brought them down onto the imaginary head in front of me as quickly as I could; and within the confines of my three feet by three feet 'stage'. The old codger in the wig and ermine pyjamas once again looked down at me over the top of his gold-rimmed half-moon glasses.

'Was it a large shovel?' he enquired, sounding like he'd chucked a couple of glass marbles into his mouth at breakfast time.

'Whit??' I thought. 'How many times had this old custard cream been to B&Q I wondered? What did he mean by a *large* shovel?'

I felt like answering, 'Naw, it was the kind you see kids using at the beach to fill their plastic bucket with sand, ya auld mental case!' But I decided not to, just in case he held me in contempt of court!

'It was the sort of shovel that you would expect to see men using to mix concrete on a building site, sir.' was my genuine answer.

He was probably none the wiser but he nodded his head regardless and motioned to the procurator fiscal to carry on as he continued to write down his notes. After a few minutes being grilled by the 'good guy', it was now the turn of the 'wank' to question me.

'No further questions my Lord.' stated the fiscal and sat down.

Campbell's defence lawyer stood up to cross-examine me. I watched as this Jacob Rees Knob lookalike stood up and walked towards me like a skinnier, shorter, effeminate Perry Mason. He had clearly been bullied at school and had now risen through the ranks of the legal fraternity to secure his place as a 'bigwig'. This wee titan tosser was now going to flex his intellectual muscles and attempt to take his evil out on my arse.

'Gulp!' I thought.

'Mr Crook, you stated in your evidence that my client Mr Campbell hit his friend Mr Stevenson over the head with a shovel several times, is this correct?'

'Yes, it is.' I answer.

'I put it to you, that they were good friends and that it was in fact banter, horseplay and youthful exuberance that they were both displaying.' he declares with a straight face.

Bullshit, I thought. If that was what *he* termed horseplay, then this wee barrister was harder than he looked!

'No, it was more than a bit of horseplay, sir. I do accept that they may have been friends but it was a violent attack in which another inmate sustained a serious concussion.' I reply, confidently.

'You said in your statement that you and your colleague both ran over to them, is this correct?'

'That's correct, yes.' I answer.

'When you got there, did you see any marks or cuts evident on Mr Stevenson's head that would've been sustained as a result of these alleged blows?' he asked.

'I never saw any actual cuts, no.' I answered emphatically.

The wee chap slams his notebook onto the desk in front of him in a futile attempt at intimidation.

'Do you actually expect his lordship, myself and the rest of this court to believe your version of events, officer Crook; that my client hammered his friend over the head with a shovel THREE TIMES yet you say there were no cuts?? I put it to you officer Crook that you are in fact lying to this court today!'

Even the sound of him calling me officer CROOK made the hairs on my neck tingle with mortification, and I already felt defeated because my name was funny for my occupation!

I replied with, 'No, I'm not lying. I didn't say that there weren't any cuts, just that I couldn't . .'

He jumps in quickly before I have a chance to complete my sentence.

'You couldn't see any cuts? Oh? I thought that you were a trained observer Mr Crook? You say that my client hit Mr Stevenson over the head with a shovel several times yet you didn't see any cuts? Prison officers are supposed to be able to notice these sorts of things are they not? What's your excuse, huh?' he asks me, with an air of superiority.

'Well, there was so much blood on Mr Stevenson's head, face and body that it was impossible to see any actual cuts on his head.' I answer, trying to conceal my contentment.

There really wasn't any defence he could've made for Campbell, it was a banged to rights case in which two screws witnessed one con thrashing another over the head with a shovel. He was as guilty as a puppy sitting next to a pile of poo! Case closed.

Obviously feeling like the prize plum he was, the defence lawyer says, 'No further questions my Lord.' as he sheepishly sits down. The judge looks at me again over the rim of his glasses and informs me that I may step down from the witness box.

Phew, my ordeal was over!

Outside the courtroom I met up with my mate, Ronnie, who had already given his evidence. We were chatting about our experience for a few minutes when the fiscal walks over to inform us that the case had been dismissed because Mr Stevenson, who had earlier in the month been released from prison, had failed to appear. I couldn't have given a hoot either way.

Not my circus, not my monkeys!

PLAYING SPOONS IN THE VISIT ROOMS

Visiting time at Barlinnie was the highlight of my day. Separated by glass screens exactly like you see in the movies with each prisoner sat inside an enclosed booth awaiting their respective visitors. There was a member of staff appointed to the visitors' side and usually because I was the rookie, it was me who drew the short straw. I really didn't mind at all as it felt more relaxed and normal on the public side of the glass and I preferred that to being stuck in the fish tank. So called because of 360° wraparound glass in the area and I guess the resemblance to Guppy's at feeding time was factored in also. It smelled like a fish tank in there too sometimes!

The huge pile of visitor passes would be given to me by the senior officer who passed them through a small hatch at the end of the screened corridor. I would take the bundle of papers and walk down the 40 or so yards to the visitors waiting area and shout out the names of the prisoners of whom they had came to see.

'SMITH, DAVIDSON, FORSYTH, MACDONALD, MACKAY...'

I paused for a nanosecond as I could see the next few names on the pile of visit passes that my colleagues had carefully organised them into a special sequence for me. Without a flinch and with no hint at a smile I instantly composed myself and read out the next batch of genuine names on the list,

'DARLING, LOVE, BAULDY, BAYNE'

Greg, the big bawheid at the desk, had deliberately put them in that order to get a laugh me. I could see some of the visitors smiling as they filed past me to take their seat in the visitor booth. I just smiled back politely, if only they knew that my name was Crook.

That was the easy bit. The biggest problem we faced was getting them all back out again after the designated time was up. They would be still sitting chatting after repeated yells of,

'RIGHT LADIES AND GENTS, THAT'S YOUR TIME UP NOW, FINISH OFF YOUR VISITS, PLEASE!'

Even on the inside of the fish tank the inmates would be dragging their heels; they would be only standing up but not walking away. Time was ironically short though as we only had a few minutes turn around before I had to start calling out more nutty names that signalled the start of another session of visits.

Visits these days aren't like that. They take place in open visit rooms where visitors and prisoners all sit around café style tables, where they can embrace and talk freely without the aid of an amplified mesh screen. This new format presented a completely different set of problems though as you might appreciate, like drugs and other contraband being passed over to the inmates. Even with closed circuit TV cameras pointed at every table and in all directions it was like something from a George Orwell novel. Prisoners and their visitors would be relentless in their efforts to try and smuggle goodies in. I remember the phone would ring and a big brother like voice from the CCTV room would announce,

'That rocket at table four has just had something passed to him by his visitor!'

It was even known for visitors to conceal contraband inside their child's nappy as a way of passing over drugs, I mean who's going to stop a guy hugging his wean?

I remember one incident where an inmate and his visitor were saying their goodbyes. They were taking a bit longer than the usual 'quick peck' so it drew the attention of the visit room officers and it became apparent that they were up to something. Open-mouthed kissing is not allowed at the visits for obvious reasons and here they were; 'haud it and daud it', almost poking their tongues down each other's throats as she tried to pass a large lump of cannabis resin to the guy. They might have gotten away with it too if it weren't for the simple fact that the visit room staff *knew* that the woman was his Mum. What a pair of inappropriate desperados!

A few years later when I was working in Glenochil Prison visits. The category of the jail had only been changed a matter of weeks and the staff, who up until then had been dealing with under 21 year old boys, were suddenly confronted with men older than they were. Some inexperienced officers were totally unprepared for the daily confrontation they faced when working with long-term adults.

An example of the staff's innocence happened one afternoon when two officers were at the desk on the main visit room door. I happened to be passing through on my way to the estates yard when I got caught up in an incident that is burned in my memory. At the farthest table in the corner a prisoner had his girlfriend, or at least a woman who was signed in as his girlfriend, sitting on his knee. Not really allowed but the two young officers seemed to be unconcerned about that until someone pointed out what they were doing! She had her baggy cotton skirt 'howked up' over her thighs, straddling the guy as they slowly and very gently rocked back and forth. They could've been spoon-feeding each other cocaine for all the staff seemed to be noticing.

'In the name of Ken Dodd's dad's dug!' I thought, I wasn't getting much of that action at home and this dude was in prison and going at it like the Easter bunny on Viagra!

It wasn't only visitors that the cons in Glenochil were caught shagging. One story in particular stands out from the others because it involved a prisoner with a female member of staff.

My mate Merv, who worked in procurement, was at his computer when the senior stores officer, Bert, came into his office and casually announces, 'I've just seen Lillian bent over a pallet, getting pumped by our passman!'

Apparently, Bert had gone into the back store area for some reason and there they were, brazenly at it. He was so embarrassed he didn't know how to respond so he just walked out again after the pair were startled by him.

Bert: 'They just looked flushed and immediately sorted themselves and pulled up their clothing as soon as they saw me!'

Merv: 'I bet they fuckin' did!'

Poor Lillian was later suspended from duty; I'm not aware of what happened to the prisoner but you couldn't blame the guy. He was offered sex from a fit young female officer while he was inside serving a lengthy prison sentence; he wasn't about to knock *that* back, was he?

Merv told me that in the months leading up to that day, they were both continually making sexual innuendos towards each other and it was obvious there was some chemistry between them. The song 'Everywhere' by Fleetwood Mac was in the charts at that time and Merv said it must have been 'their song' as they both used to sing to each other, 'I wanna be with you everywhere', whenever it came on the radio in the office. How to draw attention to yourselves or what?

A few weeks later around half a dozen of us were on our way into the jail for the start of our shift and the unfortunate Lillian was right there in the pedestrian lock alongside us. The governor had most likely called her in to officially let her go, I'm not sure. Nobody said a word; we were all just stood there, red-faced, waiting for what seemed like eternity for the inside door to be unlocked. A pile of daily newspapers was stacked up at the gate ready to be distributed to various cellblocks.

Right there on the top was a National daily Redtop carrying the headline, "LUSTY LIL!"

NAE TELLY AND LORRAINE KELLY

When I first arrived at Her Majesty's Young Offenders Institution and Detention Centre Glenochil in February 1987, it was a far cry from the bleak Victorian jail that I had left behind in Glasgow. For a start this was a newer establishment with a much more modern feel to it and housed Young Offenders and Detention inmates.

Detention was distinctly separate from the regular Young Offenders and provided 16 to 21 year olds with a 'short sharp shock' punishment given out as a deterrent and alternative to a regular prison sentence. Inmates were treated like national service recruits from the nineteen fifties and drilled every day like wee tin soldiers. Lavish items like televisions were absent and they were forced to polish up their boots to a high gloss and marched at the double everywhere they went, even if it was only to the toilet blocks. They were then given the luxury of two minutes to 'SOAP ON!' and then a further two minutes to 'SOAP OFF!' again, before being marched outside to the parade ground for endless hours of square-bashing and more ego-destroying demoralisation meted out to them by a sergeant- major type screw. Brutal stuff which fairly dampened any 'cardboard gangster' aspirations … for a wee while.

Detention was designed to scare the living bejeezus out of the boys and prevent them from re-offending; with the express intention of making them believe that this was what adult prison was actually like, which of course it wasn't. This form of punishment was discontinued in the 1990's when the authorities revealed that fundamentally, it didn't work.

The first pair that came into my new painting and decorating workparty were two young inmate's aptly nicknamed Jinky and Coco. Young guys like this were volatile and very unpredictable. I could be standing a few yards from them and they would start shouting and swearing at each other, then their fists would start to fly.

They could be punching lumps out of each other totally oblivious to where they were and I would shout,

'Hey you two, put away the handbags before you chip your nail varnish!'

This would normally be enough to break the tension and they would start laughing and see sense. This pair were stupider than Jupiter. Wee Coco started telling us this mad story one morning how he'd heard another inmate talking about his grandma and her semtex, when he was corrected by his pal.

"Naw Coco, ya daft cunt, he was talking about grammar and syntax coz he's in full-time education, where you should be!" roared Jinky with laughter.

At that time, there was a particular sentence handed down to young offenders for Capital offences. Instead of being sentenced to Life like adult inmates, Young Offenders were ordered to be detained at 'Her Majesty's Pleasure'. Coco had been ordered to serve his sentence at Her Majesty's Pleasure. You would think that the Queen had better things to do than sit with a list of teenagers' names and whispering to herself, 'Should One let this little brat out of jail this year? I don't think so, Coco!'

I had a civilian painter employed on a temporary contract working with my squad too and Bobby was a gem of a guy. He was an Alloa man in his late fifties with good humour and humility too. The inmates warmed to him immediately, it was impossible not to. He would concoct the usual workplace scenarios like sending one of our young inmates to the stores to ask for a kettle of steam, a tin of tartan paint or a glass hammer. The boys loved his banter and it helped the day pass so much quicker for them. Laughing was always at the heart of our day, laughs like the day we were working in the prison kitchen. We were repainting the storage areas when the catering officer came through and asked if any of us wanted some pizza, as there were loads leftover and about to be binned. Never one's for refusing food, Bobby and I took the two young inmates through to the serving area where we were handed four cheese & tomato pizzas. Picking up a circular pizza cutter, I asked young Coco if he wanted his pizza cut into four slices or eight, to which Coco replied,

'Better make it four, I don't think I could eat eight slices.'

It suddenly dawned on me why he might've been nicknamed Coco!

Everything seemed to be going fine and I was settling in well at Glenochil. I very quickly discovered however that within a few months of my arrival, the category of the place was to be changed from a Young Offenders establishment (Y.O.'s) into a long-term adult prison. Not surprisingly, just as I was getting used to working with young offenders, the Scottish Office decide to change everything. Here were some of the same adult prisoners whom I had left in Barlinnie just six months earlier, following me to my new jail. This was turning into Groundhog Day. It was actually a blessing for me, as by this time I had my own workparty that provided a much sought after job for inmates and we would carry out essential maintenance using prisoner labour. I quickly realised that adults were much more productive when it came down to a work ethic. If you have ever had teenage kids you will be aware of how lazy they can be sometimes? Just like Young Offenders, there are many parallels to be drawn between them!

I had a small squad of about half a dozen inmate painters and we would work together as a team, developing a rapport and getting to know each other on a personal level. Guys would tell me stuff that they would never divulge to other screws, because basically I don't think they really classed us as prison officers. Working within the painting squad was a far more relaxed regime from the one they had experienced down in their cellblocks. The attitude of Estates staff was more conducive to the building site than the Army parade ground, therefore it was a much sought after job for prisoners.

Glenochil Prison had four main halls named Alpha, Bravo Charlie and Delta. I'm not aware of who made up the names for these halls, but let's agree that he wasn't the most imaginative dude in the world. The four halls were each joined together by a very long, 400-metre corridor running the entire length of the cellblocks, which the previous young offender inmates had imaginatively christened 'The Russian Front'. It had been painted in a brightly coloured abstract pattern and the design had apparently been copied from an airport departure lounge somewhere. Research had claimed that it had a calming effect.

Aye right! Who had sold them on that idea, I wondered, Del Boy Trotter?

No sooner were the adult prisoners all settled nicely into Glenochil, than we had one almighty RIOT. Lucky white heather, I thought. I have only been in the job three years and already I've been in two riots! This one, like the earlier riot at Barlinnie, also involved hostages and was very nasty as one officer almost lost an eye. The entire place was smashed up with most prisoners destroying their own cell after being locked up for 24 hours a day. Most cell windows had been smashed too which meant each inmate was then exposed to the elements, not very wise.

Even though inmates are entitled to an hours' exercise each day, under the circumstances this wasn't going to happen as apparently they'd had plenty exercise whilst smashing up their cells to last them a month or two. Every day there were serious incidents and dozens of prisoners had gone on dirty protests where they smeared themselves and their cells in faeces because of the conditions in which they had forced themselves to live. You could almost smell the irony! A squad of officers with the call sign, 'Tango-Golf 99' were continually on stand by dressed in full riot gear and nicknamed 'The Armadillos'. So-called because of the ninja-turtle like armoured-padding outfit that they wore all day every day. They would don their helmets and grab a shield each whenever the shout came.

If an alarm bell had gone off these guys would be there in seconds to quell the melee.

Prisons are, by their very nature, extremely violent places as one would imagine. Assaults happen with astonishing regularity, with an officer or inmate being assaulted every hour of everyday somewhere on the UK prison estate. During the lockdown/special measures at Glenochil, the media took a keen interest in the goings on in the jail and cameras and reporters seemed to be set up at the end of the driveway to the prison in perpetuity.

I remember being sent outside to guard the exterior perimeter when Glenochil was put on Amber Alert. TV cameras and reporters were everywhere as usual. A couple of officers from the estates unit and myself were standing chatting outside the fence when lights and a television camera crew appeared about fifty yards from where we were standing. A young reporter was standing doing her piece to camera using us guys as her background.

When she had finished her live broadcast the lights were switched off and she made her way over to speak to us. She asked me what it was like working down in the cellblocks. I told her that the smell wasn't too pretty and joked that I would much rather be doing her job. She laughed before adding rhetorically and in a polite voice,

'They really are a shower of shite aren't they?'

I recognised the reporter as a very young Lorraine Kelly. I wonder if she remembers?

Such a large percentage of the cellblocks had been destroyed that the entire establishment was to be given a complete overhaul. One block at a time was closed down and the prisoners transferred to other prisons around the country. The renovation work took years to complete and was carried out by external contractors working alongside prison staff and ironically, inmates too. My small squad of inmate painters had been joined by a couple of local civilian painters who were employed by Marshall Construction of Alloa on a permanent loan.

Jimmy Scobbie and Bobby Craig were a lot older than me and the inmates took to them really well, as they were a proper double act. They would occasionally share their sandwiches with the squad and leave them biscuits etc bought from the prison shop, so they were a big hit.

Jimmy would tease the prisoners and Bobby would wind them up too and they weren't afraid to stand up for themselves either. These two men had more aptitude for working with criminals than a lot of screws that I had came across. I loved working with them both and I miss Jimmy dearly, as sadly he died of cancer a few years later. Jimmy and Bobby had worked with my squad and me for over five years.

The 'Estates' block where my painting workshop was located also had a well-equipped engineering shed, where I first met a civilian contractor named Campbell Baxter. Campbell had earned the fabulous nickname 'two soups'!

There was an electricians unit, a plumbing and heating section and a joiner's workshop. We also had a civilian plasterer whom the inmates had christened 'Crocodile Dunderheid' because he was crazy enough to gut animals in the works yard that he had shot on some fancy Lairds estate the previous weekend. He was a nice fella though and took the ribbing well. Real name Rab, he was the walking double of Seth, the old shepherd character from the ITV soap, Emmerdale; he even owned a similar deerstalker type cap and sported the same large grey handlebar moustache!

'Here comes John the Crook!' he'd announce as I approached, before giggling in a high-pitch maniacal laugh. Rab was as daft as a brush and was heavily involved in the hunting, shooting and fishing scene. He regularly used to bring bags of rabbits, trout and pheasant into the yard to skin, gut or pluck them. Some of the less far travelled prisoners from the inner city areas thought that this was great and these weekly blood and guts fests were, more likely than not, the only real wildlife that they had clapped eyes on. The contradiction being, that the wildlife was in fact dead!

When I first took over the painting workshop it had been ran by Roland, the incumbent officer, who was being transferred back to discipline duties once I was in post. A civilian painter, Ian Paterson, who had worked in Glenochil for about twenty years, had been Roland's faithful sidekick. He lived in Tillicoultry and took me under his wing, so to speak. Ian really made me feel welcome in the place and he would explain everything I needed to know about procedures, the stock card system, ordering materials, etc. Ian was very easy to like and I used to drop him off at the pub near my house at lunchtime and pick him back up again. He had a drink problem and was, if I dare suggest it, a functioning alcoholic. One morning I opened the metal container that we used as a paint store to find Ian with a can of super lager at his lips, mid gulp. Alcohol is forbidden in a jail as you might well imagine and Ian was mortified; I just said something like,

'Hurry up and finish that, I hope you don't have a second one hidden anywhere, Ian?'

He looked sheepish and said he was sorry. 'Aye, for getting caught!' I told him.

We both laughed and the incident was never mentioned again. I loved Ian; he was just the nicest old fella.

Located in the estates block was a shower and toilet area and in the toilet cubicle was a piece of white melamine measuring around two feet by two feet. Lying beside the board was a soft thick joiners pencil, ideal for doodling cartoon sketches, poems and limericks on the aforementioned whiteboard. Someone who'd wanted to encourage mischief had placed it there, namely, me! One of the engineers was a brilliant cartoonist and he would occasionally sketch other staff and inmates if an incident occurred that he could extract a joke from.

It transpired that one of the estates officers had been seen protesting outside a local carpet shop after they had kept his payment and had not supplied or fitted his carpets. He and his wife and son had stood protesting outside their shop spouting the odds about the owners being bent, until they gave him his money back. The cartoons and poems that appeared on what was now termed *The Graffiti Board*, were so funny that tracings of them were often made to preserve for posterity. Other wee silly ones would appear hastily 'sketched' by guys like me who couldn't draw if their life depended on it, but it would stir up a reaction and would be funny all the same.

One officer in particular, named Ned Roberts, was the butt of more than his fair share of the cartoons and jokes appearing on the graffiti board. Ned wasn't exactly my favourite dude at the time and his wife had become pals with my wife. He seemed to be in my face wherever I looked. I'd get in from work and he'd be sitting gossiping with the women and holding court with the kids on his knee and it just irritated me that he acted like such a dork. Ned *loved* being a screw and would still have his uniform on long after he'd finished work. I'd be outside his house at 10pm to drop off his missus who had been out with my wife, and Ned would appear at his door still in full uniform! I began to wonder if he slopped out his kids wearing pyjamas with HMP badges on the shoulders?

It grated on me that he came from Easterhouse and like me had transferred through to Glenochil only two years previously from a jail 30 miles down the M80, yet here he was talking like a highlander about the 'bairns' and 'ye ken this' and 'ye ken that'. I think Ned must've been one of those people who go to Morecambe for the September weekend and return home to Glasgow speaking with a Lancashire accent. Even the occasional inmate would say to me, 'I thought Mr Roberts came fae Glesga, John?' It was embarrassing. I did like him in the beginning and we'd had a few drinks together when I'd first arrived, but Ned's self-important sycophantic manner drove me in the opposite direction and we ended up not even speaking to each other by the time I left.

I was beginning to discover that most of the inmates who came through my workparty over the years were actually good fun once I got to know them. I was enjoying my new work setting, finding out what made inmates tick and accepting them as everyday people; almost forgetting that they were convicts was a novel concept for me. They would speak to me in the same way that they spoke to each other and vice versa. What I mean is, they appeared to subliminally forget that I was a screw, which was odd. So much so that they would just come out with verbal platitudes before they had a chance to realise where they were. It was funny sometimes.

Bobby and I had nicknamed our three current passmen 'Hughie, Louie and Dewy' and they were scraping and undercoating metal railings right beside us, when Louie pipes up, 'Ah wiz as high as a giraffe's arse last night, that was some strong fuckin' blaw big Shug had, wasn't it Dewy?'

Dewy turned to look at me, as he suddenly realised where they were. I raised my head and stared at Louie with one corner of my mouth rising towards my left eye in a sardonic semi-smile. Louie's face turned red, he was mortified when he became conscious I was there. He didn't know where to look.

He probably thought that I could send him for a drug test, but I just laughed it off and teased him about it. I didn't want to set a precedent of fear and create an atmosphere within the workparty; that would only make them reluctant to talk freely and I might lose all face, as well as an abundant source of future writing material. Besides, it was hardly the crime of the century and was something that I wouldn't have knocked back myself if the time and place were right!

This stance paid off for me on numerous occasions as prisoners saw me as someone whom they could trust and confide in. Several of them had approached me throughout the years to 'tip me off' if something serious was about to go down. They also had enough faith in me to seek out my ear whenever they felt vulnerable or needed guidance. Hughie Louie and Dewy, and indeed most of my workparty over the years, would talk freely to me about their crimes, past and present, and I used to hear first hand accounts straight from the horses mouth as it were about drug raids, armed robberies, frauds, embezzlements and even murders; all very fascinating and gory stuff.

Everyone was opening up to me so much that I was beginning to feel like the prison agony uncle!

MY BAD LUCK ON A DUMPER TRUCK

One fella who worked in my workparty, even had the CCTV photographs of himself committing an armed robbery at his local Building Society branch in Dumbarton. His lawyer had supplied him with these 'stills' and they had been productions at his recent trial where big Kenny Monaghan had been sentenced to a total of 10 years for armed robbery and other offences he had committed previously. He got away with little over a grand but was caught three months later in Blackpool; a haven for mad Scottish robbers, most of them owning B&B's and guesthouses... JOKING!

We used to sit in my workshop and just chat some days; and at tea breaks we would do the crossword in the newspaper. Kenny was very personable and he could uncannily tease information from you without you even being aware that you were telling him anything of note. He would often say things to me gleefully like, 'I'm serving a ten stretch, John, for stealing the equivalent of your monthly pay packet.'

'Who the hell had told *him* how much I earned?' I thought.

On the particular afternoon that Kenny had committed his offence, he'd been out of his face on prescription medication, he told me, and lay hidden in bushes watching the door of the Nationwide Building Society. He'd had a last minute brainwave to go in and rob it when the place had emptied of customers, but before it had actually closed its doors for the day. Kenny hadn't planned this too well though, as he never brought a weapon or a mask with him, so he sat in the bushes cutting the sleeve off his loose knit pullover to use as a face screen and whittling a weapon from a small tree branch. He then frantically scribbled a demand note on a piece of scrap paper that said,

'THIS GUN IS LOADED - PUT ALL THE CASH YOU HAVE INTO THIS PLASTIC BAG - DON'T TRY AND BE A HERO OR YOU'LL BE A DEAD ONE!'

The poor woman was hysterical and was so terrified that she grabbed fistfuls of notes, stuffing them frantically into the Tesco bag that Kenny had kindly supplied for her. She hadn't even noticed that the gun shape that she could see through his jumper was in actual fact, just a whittled twig. He was chased through the side streets and across an electrified railway line by cops, eventually hiding in the space between two couplings of a freight train that eventually travelled all the way to the north of England. He almost died of hypothermia!

The CCTV pictures that he showed me were hilarious though, because in the first one it is evidently *him* entering the branch as his vacant-looking face can clearly be seen looking straight at the camera. The next still is a wide-angled shot where Kenny is holding the makeshift balaclava made from his pullover in his left hand and a small wooden 'gun' in the right. The third photograph shows him pulling the jumper sleeve over his now well-kent face. He explained to me that he couldn't see where he was going, so he left the mask off until he got to the teller's window! The photographs looked like something from a Marx Brothers movie *and* they were in black & white too. Kenny was laughing like a tickled toddler as he was showing them to me. He had served lots of time over the years he told me and his nickname was big Schizo, I didn't need to ask why! All of this makes him sound like a disturbed, dangerous madman, but while he was in jail he was a big sensitive soul and would sob at the least wee thing. The following story is a fine instance of our officer inmate relationship.

One afternoon I took Kenny, who was now a category C, outside the jail with me in the dumper truck to collect bags of sand, which were left at the officers' quarters after a flood. We both loaded all the sandbags into the front of the dumper and the bold Kenny then asked me if he could have a go at driving the dumper; in a momentary lapse of concentration and/or common sense, I said yes! Kenny was like a big kid who had been given the keys to his dad's car as he raced to grab the steering wheel. In his excitement to drive, he hadn't noticed that I was still standing on the platform at the rear of the truck and as he pulled forward with a sudden jerk, I was thrown backwards and landed full-force onto the tarmac straight onto my back. As I lay there motionless and screaming in agony, Kenny performed an emergency stop that would have put any driving examiner through the windscreen, if the dump truck had one. He jumped out of the seat and ran over to me so concerned that I was badly hurt and with tears running down his face, tried to pick me up and carry me back to the prison gatehouse. He was such an emotional big guy. Many inmates would have taken this opportunity to escape while their jailer lay motionless on the floor, but that obviously hadn't crossed Kenny's mind, as he seemed more concerned for me! I went to the prison health centre and the doctor gave me some painkillers and sent me home for the rest of the day. When I returned to work the following morning big Schizo was waiting to ask me,

'What painkillers did they give you?'

'The doctor gave me half a dozen DF118's but after taking two I felt sick so I binned them.' I told him.

'Fuck sake man, they're worth a fiver each doon the hall, John!' yells Kenny, as he proceeds to rummage through the bin in our office looking for the remaining four tablets!

'I think you misunderstand big fella' I told him, laughing. 'Not *that* bin, my kitchen bin at home!'

I heard from a colleague many years later, sadly, that Kenny had died of acetaminophen poisoning following a paracetamol overdose. It seemed a tragic waste of a life as I had witnessed so much good in him. I can't help but wonder whether he would still have been a career criminal had he been brought up in different surroundings.

Our background and our genes, nature/nurture and all that, shape us; and our personality is usually determined within the first five years of life. I like to suppose that big Kenny and I might have been good friends had we met under different circumstances? He certainly left a huge impression on me as a fellow human.

There were some very seriously sick men with whom I spent a lot of my days with too. I hadn't exactly led a sheltered life before I worked in the SPS but some of the stories I heard were shocking, even to me. What some humans were capable of doing to each other was just truly breathtaking.

I had a guy working with me for a short while who had been sent to Glenochil whilst awaiting assessment for The State Hospital at Carstairs. His name wasn't Drake, but that's what we shall call him for the purposes of this story. He was about six foot four wearing only his socks and weighed about seventeen stones with shoulders as wide as a transit van; a man mountain right enough. He had been heavily sedated on Largactil, an anti psychotic drug, at the start of his sentence and recently his dose was reduced to allow his reintegration to the mainstream. Inmates on this type of medication were frequently seen walking around like zombies. So much so that the staff used to call this the Largactil Shuffle. Drake's mental health was still in very poor shape and the other members of my squad were terrified of him; let's just say that Drake was 'a great bunch of guys' and leave it at that.

While we were having our tea break one afternoon, we both sat across from one another in my office at the painters' workshop and Drake, apropos of nothing, starts talking to me like we were just two pals having a blether. He asks me if I want to know his story.

'If you feel that you want to talk about it?' I reply, without giving the game away that I was desperate to hear it, especially from him!

His eyes were matt, almost black, and showed absolutely no emotion as he spoke. Him and a few of his pals were having a few cocktails at their local spit and sawdust bar in Partick in the west end of Glasgow he told me, and about half a dozen of them were sitting around a bare wooden table playing dominoes. Apparently, domino players can get really upset if anyone plays a slightly different game from the one that the group are used to playing, so let's just agree that domino players are a strange bunch. Anyway, to cut a long one short, the table gets turned upside down, the toys are thrown from the pram and the toddlers are screaming at one another. Drake and one of his neighbours, wee Brendan, are chucking double sixes at each other and all sorts of cheating accusations are thrown at Drake by his wee pal. Once things have settled down they all notice that one of the company is missing in action, it's the bold Drake. A couple of them check the powder room and another two or three of them go outside to the car park. No sign of him so they all go back inside to resume their game.

About twenty minutes pass by and the saloon doors burst open like two louvre doors in the Wild West. In storms a scary-faced Drake who swiftly challenges wee Brendan, with whom he had the earlier beef, to a fight outside and all because he had the nerve to accuse Drake of cheating at the game. Brendan follows Drake out to the car park with the rest of the group following close behind. Once they're outside Brendan makes a beeline for him, running at him like Usain Bolt. Drake swiftly grabs the handle of the large machete secreted under his coat and which he had gone home to fetch. Once Brendan is within swords length Drake rapidly draws the razor-sharp blade across Brendan's neck with such a force that it cuts his head clean off in the process!

His body though, if you know anything about the fundamental law of physics, still has forward momentum and as his head falls onto the asphalt and rolls down the car park, his body is thrust forward, the trajectory being such that it leaves Drake to reflexively catch his late friend as they both fall to the floor. Drake is now drenched in blood and partially pinned beneath Brendan's now headless bloody corpse!

To hear this coming straight from the swordsman's mouth was a very chilling experience; as my old granny said to me when I told her this story, 'That's pretty fuckin' gruesome, son!'

I was, for once in my life, completely speechless. I mean, what do you say to that? How do you react? Drake showed no emotion, save the occasional inappropriate smile, as he gave me his account. It was like he was telling me what he had just eaten for his lunch. I kept Drake on sandpapering duty and never even let him have the use of a paint scraper until he left for Carstairs. He worked with me for a few weeks but never did I come across a more frightening and intimidating individual.

JOSEPH KLOBBER THE RELUCTANT ARMED ROBBER!

I had been at Glenochil for almost two years when Joseph Klobber was allocated a job with my painting squad. He had been sentenced to 4 years for armed robbery. He was a bright guy, in his early thirties, first offender and seemed like a really decent, and surprisingly principled dude.

Joe ran a small service business, which was only just keeping him afloat. He was overheard in his local pub in Hamilton one night saying stuff about, 'Needing to get his hands on a lot of easy money!' Joe drunkenly and naively agreed to be the getaway driver in a smash and grab type robbery.

His co-accused, whom I never met, had taken him to a flat where they were to meet the planner. When Joe was introduced to this guy he didn't really trust him and had tried to back out. The dude obviously wasn't happy with this and pulled a loaded pistol on Joe, pointing the muzzle into his neck he whispers,

'Aye yer daein' it ya cunt! I know where you, yer wife and yer wean live, you'll wish the night never happened!'

Joe, who by this time was in it up to his neck, agreed and hey ho, he received a four-year stretch because there was a gun involved. He had only been in prison a matter of weeks when we met, maybe two months maximum. We used to chat for hours about normal everyday stuff and it felt refreshing that he wasn't the usual recidivist that hadn't learned anything from their seventy-five previous encounters with the penal system. He was a pleasant guy who had already felt repentant *before* he carried out his crime and in all likelihood would never offend again. I used to speak to him about what was happening with building my new house, summer holidays with my kids, etc; Joe spoke about his family and personal life too. He said his business had been doing pretty well and that he had employed a few guys too. I was impressed and asked him what had happened.

A legitimate business deal that he'd got himself involved in had gone down to the tune of tens of thousands of pounds and Joe had lost out, big time. It was the late eighties and Rave's were the big thing so he decided to stage a large event and invested a considerable sum of money on the venture. He hadn't anticipated the enormity of the project he had undertaken though. He hadn't realised just how many different agencies would be involved; Police Ambulance, public toilets, equipment hire, safety checks, stewards, licences, booking the live acts, etc. After he was made to jump through loads of hoops, he was ultimately refused the licence for the event from the council for some health and safety issue but Joe still had to pay all of his creditors, and as he hadn't taken out a cancellation insurance policy he subsequently lost all of his business profits. Ouch!

It was practically everything he had. Apart from a few old pieces of machinery and an old Ford Transit van that was on its last legs anyway. He didn't own his house, as it was the council semi he grew up in. Joe had simply taken over the tenancy agreement years before when his Mother had died. In his own words he was 'as skint as a poof's knees.'

The car stalled when he tried to screech the getaway vehicle away from the scene, as he was so nervous. They got away but only just *and* with no booty, as there coincidentally happened to be four cops coming out of the council offices across the street; what's the chances? They'd heard the alarm bell and spotted the trio running out of the jewellery shop. The police gave chase and his three accomplices dropped most of the bags. Joe and his gang got away with about five grand worth of trinkets between them, hardly a successful job. He was released on parole after about a year working with me and I never saw or heard anything more about him. This was sadly the case with most inmates; I mean, who is going to contact the jail to let you know how they're getting on? That's the sort of thing we do with schoolteachers, but not screws, is it? Well, as it happens, it has now been around six months since I started writing Joe's particular story and I have dropped back in here to update it. Yesterday I received a private message from a woman on Facebook. She apologised for the intrusion and asked if I was the same John Crook whom her husband had spoken so fondly of from his time spent in jail? She said that he thought he'd recognised my profile photo but wasn't sure as it had been 25 years since he last saw me. It was Joe's wife! Once she had told me his name, I said that I indeed remembered him. She told me that he'd always appreciated that I'd spoken to him like a regular person and hadn't judged him or made him feel small in any way. I was touched that Joe had remembered me being such a positive influence. His wife said he was grateful to me for showing him chords on his guitar and that jail time could've been a lot worse if it hadn't been for my attitude towards him. She joked that he had never returned for a sleepover! Joe sent me a friend request on Facebook, which I accepted and we agreed to meet up at some point for a beer.

Arranging to meet up for beers with someone who actually spent time inside with you is one thing, meeting someone accidentally that recognised you from prison when beers are involved, and you could have an entirely different scenario on your hands.

I was singing and playing guitar in a duo around 1997. We were doing a gig in a wee packed bar in the centre of Stirling called Drouthy Neeburs. We had only played about three songs when a guy standing over at the bar kept staring at me, but I never reacted to his somewhat relentless gaze. Somewhere between Del Amitri and R.E.M. the bar manager Vinny walks over to me and hands me a pint of my tipple of choice at the time.

'Thanks mate, who bought me that?' I asked him.

Vinny looked over towards the fella at the bar who by this time was walking towards the exit and waving at me. I waved back at him as Vinny told me, 'That big fella sent it over for you, John, he said that he remembers you from Glenochil.'

I then recognised him as a notorious gangster from Fife who was only in my workparty for a short time. That could've been a whole lot worse. I would imagine if the guy had been a total raging space cadet, instead of being sent a pint I could've been sent to A&E. Or if I'd walked around Glenochil with an attitude like Jack McGill from the Bar-L earlier in my time, even the most benign of prisoners would find it difficult to stop themselves from panning my melt in with one of the guitars before finishing me off with a microphone boom stand!

TWISTS AND TURNS WITH BIG WILLIE BURNS

I first met Willie Burns when he was in the 'Digger', a colloquialism for the punishment/isolation block. According to the staff that worked with him in there, he was a 'big lanky Glaswegian with a temper like a tannedarsed toddler. He earned the nickname *Vaseline* behind his back, and he hated it. If Willie Burns had heard anyone calling him Vaseline he would've set them alight and put the flames out with his fists!

One of the digger screws told me, 'You just have to look at him the wrong way and he'll be in your face like a swarm of angry wasps with chilli stuck to their arses!' They said he was one of the most aggressive prisoners they had in the place.

Two civilian painters and myself had been working in the digger for a day or so repainting some of the cells. Taking our squad of prisoner labour in there with us wasn't permitted because of the sensitive nature of the place. The staff that regularly worked in the digger were dressed in protective riot gear, as there was every chance of being attacked and assaulted by the prisoners held in there. We had our nice clean white bib & brace overalls and a jumbo roller to protect us!

I had been working for almost an hour when I heard this muffled voice from behind one of the locked doors shouting through the tiny gap.

'Here boss, could you get me a job working with you?'

Willie said he was a painter, like most of the inmates who were trying to impress me, had claimed. I was more concerned as to the reason *why* he was in the digger? I asked the unit staff and they said he was there to keep him away from the mainstream. He was a troublemaker and he did lose the plot sometimes they said, but he had quietened down since being transferred into their section. I told

Willie that I hadn't much influence over who came to work with me, that was the job of the allocation board but I would speak to them if he wished.

I don't know why but I kind of felt sorry for him. He was outwardly very extrovert and mouthy but I sensed that hiding behind that gossamer-thin veneer of self-confidence, was a vulnerable wee boy with no feeling of self-worth. I found him interesting. He was extremely likeable, and his demeanour once you got to know him was charming in the extreme. Just don't upset him for god's sake! If only one knew exactly what upset him though? He would keep Bobby, Jimmy and me entertained with his banter through our few days working there and eventually I decided to speak to the labour allocation board on his behalf.

'You'd better not let me down Willie. I'll be disappointed if you do mate' I told him as he strolled into my workparty two weeks later.

'I won't boss. I had to get oot that place coz the screws were doing my fuckin' nut in!' say's the bold Vaseline, ignoring the fact that I too, was one of them screw types as well.

He used to make me giggle like a big school lassie most of the day you couldn't help yourself. He would do impersonations of other cons *and* staff including myself. His routines were as good as any skits Rory Bremner might have done and sometimes he could be rather cutting.

Which brings me perfectly to his crime!

Willie, like most of the guys I worked closely with over the years, told me his story of how he wound up in jail. He said he had been in his local kebab takeaway in Maryhill ordering his favourite munch box. The place was busy when he starts arguing with the guy on the till over the amount of change he'd been given. Willie is losing it massively and it's not long before he lets his fists fly. The guy behind the till gets the better of him so Willie skitters away up the road to procure a 'chib' and returns to the shop to take his evil revenge out on the fella with a kitchen boning knife. When the red mist cleared, the police had Willie in the back of the meat-wagon, his victim already half way to hospital with a kidney falling out of a huge gash on the left side of his lower back!

He was initially charged with attempted murder. His lawyer though, had managed to get the charge reduced to assault to severe injury and permanent disfigurement and he was jailed for two and a half years.

Who was his lawyer I wondered? Rumpole of the Bailey??

If big Vaseline had fallen into the Clyde, he'd emerge with a salmon in each pocket and a laminated 'Get Out Of Jail Free' card, signed by wee Betty Windsor herself!

IT WASN'T MY FAULT HE DIDN'T LIKE SALT!

It was late January in 1992 when I started working with Arnie Black, a well-spoken man from the south side of Glasgow. He was around thirty-five years old, five-foot seven but very well built. He wore round wire-rimmed glasses that gave him an intelligent appearance way beyond his schooling. Arnie was very unassuming and never said much in company; but like the adage goes, 'never judge a book by its cover'.

We had been working together for about two weeks rolling and brushing white emulsion onto the dining hall ceilings. We had the radio playing in the background and Arnie was singing like a canary, telling me this story about a guy he went to school with, who was sentenced to life with a tariff of twenty years. I was so impressed by Arnie's storytelling ability and the way he drifted from one layer of the tale to the next. This guy was better at building suspense than Tolkien!

'My best friend lived with his Dad', Arnie told me. 'Let's call him *Wee Salty* for reasons that will become apparent!' he smirked.

Wee Salty's parents owned a cottage in the Shawlands area of Glasgow that had a licenced grocers shop attached, and they had done rather well for themselves over the years. His mother had also recently died and his dad had been awarded a massive insurance payout. The figure was impressive. So much so, that when Salty caught a glimpse of his fathers' latest bank statement, he thought he had hit the jackpot! Only one snag though, it wasn't his money.

He had to find a way of getting his grubby wee paws on that balance!

His late grandfather had established the business in 1948 before it was subsequently transferred to his dad in the Seventies so it shouldn't have been a surprise to him that it had accumulated as much. £475k was the available balance and wee Salty was just desperate to make a withdrawal.

He had seen where his father had kept his wallet and had intended stealing it when the appropriate opportunity arose. He waited until his father was asleep before he made his move; only, he wasn't going for the bankcard. He was looking for the telephone banking details which he knew his poor old dad had kept written down on a piece of paper folded up inside the zipped section of his wallet as he had a memory like a goldfish.

Once he had the numbers and passwords, Salty dialled the telephone banking service every couple of nights over the next week. He pretended to be his dad and transferred all of the balance in large chunks into his *other* account!

He knew that at some point the new *zero balance* was going to be discovered, so he enacted part two of his cunning plan to ensure this wasn't going to cause him any problems. Wee Salty did all the cooking at home for both himself and his dad as he had once worked as a chef in a Hotel in The Trossachs and liked to *keep his hand in* so to speak.

Over the following months he slowly and systematically poisoned his poor old dad by adding carefully measured doses of common everyday salt, into all of his food and drink. His dad very quickly became too ill to open up the shop and the family doctor was baffled by his condition. Salty continued to open the greengrocers himself every morning so as not to arouse any suspicion from his customers.

Even after his dad had been admitted to hospital, Salty would be up visiting him every afternoon and evening to ensure that he had enough salty snacks to see him through to the afterlife!

He was caught a few short months later, following his father's death, when a suspicious neighbour phoned the police. Apparently she heard him arguing with a known friend on his way home from the pub late one night about the best way to murder someone. Another neighbour told cops that Salty was arguing and shouting with the guy, and bragging, 'I know how to do somebody in. I've done it before!'

The neighbours' hunch proved right, because after further investigations had been carried out, the cops had enough evidence against Wee Salty to charge him.

Apparently a lot of convicted criminals are caught out in this way, Arnie told me. He said they can't hold their water, and that urge to tell somebody is so strong, it's almost impossible not to!

The most famous case in point that I can remember was the American guy who worked for a large multi-national finance corporation and had discovered an ingenious way to make money. He noticed that the bank accounts of all the tens of thousands of investors on his client portfolio had balances that ended with the odd 'point one' of a cent. He siphoned off all those odd 'point one' cents including the interest that it had accrued into his own account. This had gone unnoticed for years.

Unfortunately for him he was caught because he blabbed to one of his associates whom he thought he could trust, but not before he had relieved his clients of hundreds of thousands of dollars by transferring their money into his own bank account with a quick stroke of his keyboard and a mere click of the mouse. If only it were that simple to make money!

A BULLET THING AND A SING WITH BING

Admissions were arriving at Glenochil reception courtesy of the police and as usual it was pandemonium. The cubicles were filling up faster than a lawyers pockets and everything was running just dandy-o. Each inmate being admitted was instructed, in turn, to place their belongings and any personal property onto the large processing table, where each item was logged and noted into the property book. Nowadays all this information would be stored on computers.

Several new recruits had started the job that week and were being shown around the prison. On this particular morning it just happened to be the reception area they were visiting, and at this the busiest of times.

A passman inmate was helping the reception staff process the admissions and had placed a large clear polythene bag with its contents plainly visible, onto the aforementioned large table. This, in full view of the assembling rookies.

"EVERYONE STAND BACK – IT'S A LIVE ROUND!" one of the newbie's exclaims!

A raw recruit leaps forward and reaches for the inmates' property bag as he continues to shout the above warning. The passman by this time had sussed what was happening and had already grabbed the 'offending article' and handed it over to the reception staff.

The senior officer who was in attendance with the rookies asked his young recruit what the problem appeared to be.

"Sir, I am ex-forces and there is a live round in that bag!" announced the rookie.

The reception officer steps forward gripping the 'live round' in his fist and as he presses a button, a small flame appears out of a hole on top of the bullet.

"Does anybody want a light?" he asks, to howls of laughter!

The reception passman was called Tommy, and said he was from Broomhouse in Edinburgh. I had noticed a lot of inmates with the letters A.C.A.B. tattooed on each knuckle and Tommy had them too. I asked him what it stood for. "All Cops Are Bastards", he answered!

Tommy was another character who had done time since he was 14 years old. He had served time in Borstal, Young Offenders and now he was in big boys prison. He was infamously quoted as the Polmont inmate, who had a verbal altercation with a generously proportioned female officer being escorted around the institution,

"Here doll, whit's your name?" asked Tommy.

"I'm not your doll, I am Miss Ireland!" she answers sternly.

Tommy quips, "Fuck me, if *you're* Miss Ireland, ah widnae like tae see the runner up!"

There are, as you already know, loads of so-called characters in jails and none so deserving of the title as my next subject.

Pat Thompson, my mad Celtic supporting ex-brother-in-law from Possilpark, Glasgow, had asked me down to a local pub in Stepps for a few beers on a warm summer night in 1994; who could say no? Pat had a pleasant nature about him with a wee bit of an edge and I liked that. Being seen around Pat usually didn't do your street cred any harm at all. But alas, Pat is not the protagonist here.

I was slaking my thirst at the bar when I noticed an ex-inmate whom I remembered from my Glenochil days, standing at the bar opposite me. He was wearing a smart leather jacket with a pale grey coloured shirt and a red tie. I recognized him as legendary bank robber turned crime author, James Crosbie, or 'Bing' to his friends. He was certainly the most intriguing and charismatic prisoner I had met to date and had many conversations with him in Glenochil when Arthur Thompson junior introduced me to him a few short years earlier. Bing had spent over 20 years behind bars, a lot of that at notorious Peterhead Jail, a cold forbidding place on the Aberdeenshire coast, where inmates and staff were perpetually locked in conflict and acrimony. James paints a very accurate picture of the place in his hilarious and hugely appealing book, 'Peterhead Porridge', available online and in all good bookstores! Bing had actually written three books after his release and when I first met him in Glenochil he was already impressing his fellow prisoners, as well as staff, with his story-telling prowess. In his younger days James moved to London and quickly got caught up in a life of petty crime. He was jailed for three and a half years for conspiracy to rob and spent his time at Verne Prison, where he made counterfeit documents for London's most celebrated gangsters, the Kray twins. But when he never got paid for the work he refused to have any more dealings with the infamous brothers. On his release he came back to Glasgow and had tried to go straight.

Back in the wee Stepps pub, my bar buddy Pat asked me who I was nodding over towards, so I told him who Bing was. By this time the ex-con was making his way through the crowd to where Pat and me were both standing. I introduced Bing to my brother in law, telling Pat, this is James, he writes books.

"I hope there's not going to be any trouble?" asked Pat, rather inappropriately!

I looked at the floor slightly embarrassed as Bing glances at him, then at me. I smile at Bing with a reassuring wink and Bing smiles back.

"Of course not," says Bing, "John and myself aren't violent people, besides, why would there be any trouble?"

"Never mind him, Bing. He has the tact and diplomacy of a toddler." I whisper. "I told Pat I knew you from work and he assumed, well, you know!"

Bing was as calm as he ever was. Smiling and telling his usual detailed laden anecdotes with panache and style. Cheaper imitations could only dream of competing with him. In the space of a few minutes he had the entire place hanging on his every word, including Pat!

Back in 1972, after carrying out a sizeable list of small heists, James Crosbie carried out Scotland's biggest bank job at the time. It was planned after he discovered a neighbour with financial difficulties had inside information about cash deliveries. Bing and an accomplice carried out the robbery at the Hillington branch of the Clydesdale Bank, easily driving away with a Scottish record haul at that time of £67,000.

A couple of years later he targeted another Clydesdale Bank, this time a branch in Whiteinch, Glasgow and broke his own record, escaping with eighty seven thousand pounds. Overnight James Crosbie became one of Britain's most wanted men. In an effort to make some fast cash to help him flee the country, he made a sizeable withdrawal, albeit illegal, from a bank in Edinburgh. The next day he was recognised by three Glasgow plain clothed officers who just happened to be in the city for a case at the high court. He was arrested leaving a pharmacy where he'd been buying paracetamol for a headache and made the front page of the papers at the time.

He pled guilty and was sentenced to 20 years. Most of this sentence was served in Peterhead Prison and the long stretch was where James found his literary skill and honed it well enough to start his writing career, writing an abundance of short stories and literary gems.

In spite of serving 12 years, his criminal career wasn't quite finished yet!

In 1996, he was arrested attempting to smuggle a quarter of a million pounds worth of cannabis through an English Airport and sentenced to another four years jail time. Then in 2000, the notorious robber was nicked once again trying to smuggle cannabis, this time he was heading into Iceland, and I don't mean the frozen food store!

A colourful character full of life and vigour, and one who could entertain, charm and beguile people as easy as smiling at them.

In January 2015, James Crosbie lost his battle with cancer and died, aged 77.

I was glad that I knew him as 'Bing'.

VILE CREATURES WITH UGLY FEATURES

Like I mentioned earlier, the violence that human beings are capable of inflicting on one another had stunned me to the core and once I got to know inmates as people, this caused real inner conflict as I grappled with my conscience. Some prisoners, whom I had previously spoken to and had actually liked, turned out to be monsters capable of the most depraved crimes.

What do you do? Start treating them differently because you learned something about them that you didn't like? Or be professional about it and act exactly the same but with a more serious non-joking manner? I began to avoid wanting to know what an inmate was in for, I left that to the curious sweetie-wummin types. I only knew what someone had done if they told me themselves or it was Jimmy Boyle! Even nowadays with so much violence and sick videos on social media, there isn't a lot that shocks me.

I know that you may be trying to conjure up an image of what some of these sick individuals actually look like, but I can assure you that they look like anyone else you would see behind the till at your local supermarket, sitting beside you on the bus or dropping their kids off at school. They do not have horns or a particular, or indeed peculiar, look about them as you might imagine. The acts that they had committed however were as depraved as you could invent in the sickest depths of your imagination.

The following accounts are examples of the sort of evil deeds committed by the most appalling individuals that I encountered during my time inside. They are in no particular order of malevolence.

Vile creature no.1

I used to see this apparition walking along the route to his workparty at the Engineers Metal Fabrication Workshop. The honey monster was about eighteen stones of blubber and he was, as my granny used to say, 'solid bone from the neck up!'

Not only had this dude fallen out of the ugly tree and hit every branch on the way down, but had fallen into the ugly puddle at the bottom! He looked like a Rhinoceros by the angle his head was to his body. His underbite was so severe he could've eaten the top part of his head with two bites. His jeans hung off his arse like a pishy nappy and I couldn't stop myself from staring at this odd looking troglodyte.

I later learned that he had taken a young nurse hostage, imprisoned her at his home in Aberdeen and then tied her up, tortured her and subsequently murdered her. He then buried the young woman in a shallow grave in his back garden. A day or so later he dug up her body and after taking her back inside the house, had raped her corpse multiple times. He was initially sentenced to Life with the recommendation that he served no less than 11 years. He must have felt that he was being treated unfairly or too severely by the court, as he thought nothing of launching an appeal against his 11 years tariff and took his case to the appeal court in Edinburgh.

The words echoing around Glenochil when he returned were, 'The big honey-monster came back with 15 years up his arse!'

Vile creature no.2

Reading electricity meters, appears on the face of it, a rather mundane, boring kind of a job? Not so for this meter reader, as he was taken hostage, tied up, severely beaten and raped!

Fresh-faced new start William had by accident, gone to the wrong house to take a meter reading and stumbled across Buster Bailey, a notorious offender. As young William was staring at the numbers on the electricity meter dials and marking his readings onto his clipboard, he felt Bailey's large and overbearing presence behind him. Turning around to find out why he was so close, he was grabbed by the older and very much stronger man and forced at knifepoint into the bedroom where a violent attack took place. William was stripped of his uniform, tied up to a chair with a thick nylon clothesline rope, and beaten around the head, body and genitals with a baseball bat and hacked at repeatedly with a kitchen meat cleaver. Bleeding from hundreds of separate knife wounds and suffering multiple bone fractures, he remembered also being raped by Bailey, as he awoke in hospital days later having been rescued by the downstairs neighbours who had heard his screams for help.

William was left tied up while Bailey had callously gone out to the pub, and on his return was greeted by a crime scene consisting of a coroner, two plain clothes detectives and four uniformed officers. What Buster Bailey's motivation was is anyone's guess. Although it was subsequently discovered that he had been pilfering electricity by rewiring his meter to bypass the system, making it look like he had been consuming very little, if any. He was only at Glenochil briefly before being moved to The State Hospital at Carstairs for assessment!

Vile creature no.3

A wee roaster from Edinburgh started working in the squad with us who had contracted H.I.V. and had then deliberately passed this on to his girlfriend. He was bragging that he had done so because she was 'messing about behind his back'. He was telling me this like he was trying to make an impression on me.

Whilst I agree that infidelity is not a very principled trait, the poor woman didn't deserve to be put 'under a sentence of death' for it, I barked at him! This was around 1988 and the treatment for H.I.V. at that time was pretty ineffective.

I also had another prisoner in my workparty who was jailed for murdering his girlfriend because she innocently gave him H.I.V. He was arguing with another inmate about his justification for killing her when one of the other cons in the workparty had shouted at him, 'Oh aye mate, that's all very reasonable behaviour, isn't it ya fuckin' steamer!'

'Right guys, let's change the subject!' I shouted.

Bobby the civilian painter leaned across to me and whispered; 'These guys heads are so far up their own arse that they're positively doughnut shaped aren't they?'

Vile creature no.4

This individual, let's call him Porky, was up there near the top of the chart. His wife had been having an affair with a fella at her work and had fallen pregnant by the colleague. She had been careless and left a pregnancy test kit in the bathroom and Porky had found the 'tell-tale wand' lying in the sink. He then started throwing the accusations at her, as they hadn't slept together in months. She confessed there and then, and they acrimoniously separated.

A couple of months later Porky drives over to the flat she had moved into with her boyfriend. Aware that she is home alone he manages to coerce her into letting him in. The conversation starts off heated and ends up with him throwing a tantrum. Angry with her for the affair, but even more angry at the fact that she's having another man's child, he loses the plot completely. He picks up a heavy marble table lamp and brings it down on her head full force. Red with rage and with astonishing cruelty, Porky then cuts the unborn foetus from his estranged wife's body!

Vile creature no.5

Some individuals do not even deserve a name.

This 'thing' had been convicted of raping an 18-month-old baby and when unable to achieve penetration, had cut her genitals open with an aluminium drinks can.

I only saw this 'creature' once as I caught a glimpse of it when I was passing its cell in Barlinnie B hall back in the mid-eighties, but the expression on its face will haunt me forever; such was my shock at reading what it had actually done!

Vile creature no.6

The last one, on this particular short list anyway, was caught coming into his work with a tobacco tin full of heroin, various pills and a bottle of vodka. He had tried to make himself a few quid by bringing them into the jail for an inmate. He was a prison officer who received four and a half years for his crime. A prisoner, who'd apparently been cut out of the deal, grassed on him and covertly the security staff had been carrying out surveillance on the officer. He was arrested at the prison gate coming into work to deliver his tracked parcel. Vile and on this list because a bent screw is a dangerous piece of work, endangering every other screws life!

LOSING FAITH IN MR GALBRAITH

I had been at Glenochil for over six years when the bombshell was dropped that our 'nice wee niche' was about to end. The SPS had decided to market test the estates function.

Some bright spark, probably at H.Q., had the nerve to think they could get the maintenance done on the cheap. This meant that outside contractors were going to be invited to tender for the work of running the maintenance function of the prison service estates. The current in-house team, i.e. us, were also invited to tender a bid. If we lost that bid we could either be absorbed back into generic prison duties again or transfer over to the new contractor. It was Hobson's choice the way I saw it so I began seeking out alternative opportunities. Meanwhile, the estates staff were advised to appoint a team to formulate a bid and it was open to all existing estates staff. The senior guys in the office were furious that us mere plebs had a chance to remove them from their lofty positions! Everyone who wanted to be considered for the Team Leader and his Deputy were invited to put their names forward.

After much debate between everyone regarding roles, I threw my hat in the ring, what had I to lose?

A few of them had said they would vote for me, because I was quite outspoken probably, and I was duly chosen as deputy. Allan Richard was voted in as Team Leader because the guys thought that he kept a cool head under pressure and he wasn't quite as much of a loose cannon as me. Allan and I were to decide between us who we wanted to assist in preparing the in-house bid. The existing management team were furious that they'd been usurped in such a brutal but in reality, impartial way, so they fought back with sleekit underhand tactics that, for them anyway, worked.

They waited until the following week when a few key mavericks were off on leave, and along with the estates boss Mr Galbraith, coerced and bullied the rest of the guys into having another vote by starting a fear campaign. They told them that the team they'd voted in weren't experienced enough and that they could all lose their jobs. Total nonsense but the sheep fell for it and a 2nd vote overturned the first one with the existing management team winning the roles.

Absolutely outrageous but that's what certain groups are like sometimes. Fickle. They can't see the wood for the trees and many of them would sell their own granny down the Clyde for the promise of that wee bit extra pudding!

I experienced a similar example of this behaviour at a union meeting in Glenochil where a proposal was put forward for debate to conference, 'That all specialist allowances be taken from existing recipients and shared equally among all prison officers.'

I was horrified that my union, the Scottish Prison Officers Association (SPOA), would accept a proposal to take payments away from some of their members! I resigned from the SPOA as a protest at their decision and held with contempt all the staff who voted for such a proposition. I felt they could have made a demand to introduce a shift allowance or similar for themselves, instead they wanted to steal *our* specialist allowance, unbelievable hypocrisy!

A further example of that, 'Fuck you jack, I'm alright!' attitude occurred when the SPS offered us an ex-gratia payment of £300 in exchange for our boot allowance which was £60 and paid twice yearly. A lot of the older guys coming to the end of their service voted to accept the offer as they would be retiring soon anyway, and it was carried. Cynically, the payment was offered and was to be paid into the Christmas wage to gain maximum effect!

Luckily, a few weeks later an officer instructor post at Cornton Vale became available. They were looking for someone to provide relief cover in the Gardens, Textiles, Laundry, Assessment, Kitchen and Vocational Training workshops. I immediately submitted my application and was invited, along with eight other applicants, for an interview three weeks later. If it weren't for the fact that one of the interviewers was a woman, I could have sworn they were the same three suits that had interviewed me for the job in Barlinnie all those years earlier; the format was exactly the same!

One of them asked me if I could drive a Tractor?

'How hard can it be?' I thought to myself. 'Yes I have driven Massey Ferguson's and John Deere heavy machinery and plant.' I answered without giving away in my expression that I had never, in actual fact, driven a tractor.

My knowledge of agricultural machinery names had been memorised the previous night because I assumed that if one of the posts I'd be covering was a gardens workparty, then it could be handy. I also took the time to learn sewing machine names and terminology and told them I had experience working with flatbeds, overlockers, bar-tackers and buttonholers!

I went on to speak about industrial laundry machines and processes, all very plausible sounding but mostly untruths and exaggerations. My pal Kevin was the officer in charge of the laundry at Glenochil, so I quizzed him beforehand. I would pick it up as I went along I thought, so only failure would come from being completely honest with the interview panel at this stage! I must have sounded convincing because the phone call came that night offering me the post. I felt like I was abandoning a sinking ship when I told the estates boss at Glenochil that I would be leaving the team to go to Cornton Vale. Mr Galbraith, the estates governor, grumbled something about bailing out on the team at such a crucial point, but it really made no difference one way or another to me, I was off to Cornton Vale.

I was only a number to Galbraith anyway and since he had been such a wee conniver over the in-house bid team selection process, I wouldn't have trusted him to tell me the right time in a roomful of clocks!

He eventually and grudgingly wished me well and I set about detaching myself from the place.

I SET SAIL FOR CORNTON VALE

It was the last week of January 1994 when I eventually managed to 'escape' from Glenochil and was delighted to be transferred to Scotland's only all-female prison, Cornton Vale. This felt like another world compared to the male establishments that I had worked in previously and it had more of a hospital feeling rather than the insane asylum atmosphere of Glenochil and Barlinnie.

The grounds were beautifully laid out with tree-lined paths, wooden benches and flowerbeds; it even had two duck ponds with real live ducks and a petting zoo! It didn't have the same *'Sword of Damocles'* feeling of impending doom about it either. I never really felt in any physical danger at Cornton Vale but it did present equally distinct experiences and challenges.

One of my first duties was an escort excursion to the new sheriff court building in Falkirk, which had been recently built. A rookie female officer, whose name was Pauline, was sent along with me and after depositing our charges with the Police in the cells area, we took the elevator up to the canteen on the top floor. It was impressive as far as lifts went, and was lined with bronzed mirrors on the walls and ceiling and had soft lighting, which gave your reflection a lovely tanned look. I pressed the shiny chrome button and we started moving. Pauline turned to me and asked in all seriousness, 'Can you imagine shaggin' in this lift?'

I smiled at her as I thought, 'Naw, but I bet *you* can!'

I had been at Cornton Vale only a matter of months when my new boss, Davy Nichols, sent me to the greengrocers in Bridge of Allan to pick up a large crate of mushrooms in the jail car. I arrived at the shop and duly asked them for the largest box of mushrooms that they had. The female assistant looked at me like I had horns.

'We usually only sell them in paper bags but a box would be prohibitively expensive.' She sneered.

'Prohibitively expensive?' I thought, what kind of mushrooms were these, psilocybin mushrooms?? We only needed them for the veggie option; we weren't having a psychedelic hippy fun day or anything like that! I told her that because of the high price, I would have to speak to my boss in Cornton Vale kitchen. It was the time before mobile phone's were widespread so she asked me if I wanted to call him, and if so I could use their phone? So with the woman right beside my ear I dialled the number and Davy answered.

'Hi David,' I started, speaking more politely than usual. 'I'm in Clive Ramsay's shop and they seem to have an issue with the mushrooms you want, apparently they are going to be quite expensive because of the quantity?'

There was a short pause and I swear I could actually hear Davy smiling widely, if that's indeed possible over a phone??

'Aye John they will be expensive!' says Davy, aware that I'm speaking politely because the woman is within earshot. 'That's because you're in the wrong fuckin' shop, it's the wee fruit & veg. shop next door you're supposed to be in, *not* Clive Ramsay's, ya big fanny!'

I had mistakenly walked into the more fancy and extortionately priced deli next door. I tried not to bite and with the same composure I answered, 'Oh, ok then David that's not a problem, I'll just be another ten minutes with them.' Again putting on my Sunday voice. As I hung up the phone, Davy was still laughing as he continued to yell light-hearted abuse at me. I informed the woman that I was meant to be in the shop next door. She just smiled and I left, mortified and red-faced.

I quickly realised that the prisoners in Cornton Vale seemed to have more of a reliance on staff, and their vulnerability was evident. I was only thirty-one and already I felt like a father figure. Not every male officer could handle this predicament. Whereas previously they had been ducking to avoid pool balls and fire extinguishers being launched at them by male inmates. In Cornton Vale they had to deal with mind games, surreptitious manipulation and sexual coercion by inmates, as well as staff.

I remember thinking at the time, that in a large percentage of these women's cases, a *man* seemed to be the main reason for them being there! Several of the women who had husbands on the outside actually had a girlfriend when inside. The prisoners called this 'Jail Bent'.

Occasionally some of these 'wee couples' would ask their unit officer if they could share a room when the numbers in the jail got really high. Cells are called rooms at Cornton Vale. At one point certain wings contained so many rooms with couples sharing, that they referred to these units as The Married Quarters. I would sometimes turn the corner of a building to be met with the vision of two inmates walking towards me hand in hand, very sweet.

That was something that I had never witnessed at any male establishment!

WITCHES AND BITCHES

My first few weeks at Cornton Vale at the beginning of 1994, was a real shock to the system as far as working relationships went. The regimes group, of which I was now a part of, was staffed entirely by female officers and I soon discovered that there were two distinct 'gangs' and I was the lone male caught in the middle!

The Witches Cauldron had four tittle-tattling gossips that took immense delight in other people's misery, especially if that person was a member of the second group. The second group, whom I have given the nomenclature, *The Chosen Ones,* also had four members and were only 'chosen' inside the envious minds of the first group.

Confused? Welcome to my world, because I was too!

In a male prison, sure we spoke about each other in a way that could be interpreted as gossip, we could be a wee bit mean about each other sometimes but we weren't spiteful; these venomous vixens however, took the blue riband. (Other cookies are available!) The Witches actually hated the Chosen Ones but were so deceitful about it that they went out of their way to be exceedingly nice whenever they met each other; they had more faces than a hexagonal town clock!

'Hiya hen, you had a good shift?' a Witch would ask a Chosen One whilst passing her in the corridor.

'Aye, it was hectic so I'm off home now to put my feet up with a glass of red!' comes the answer.

All very civilised and cordial, I thought.

A few seconds later and under her breath, Gertie, the wicked witch of the west, whispers to the rest of her cauldron,

'Hectic? She doesn't know the meaning of the word. She's fuckin' made out of porcelain and would break if she had to deal with an angry prisoner!'

Snide, vitriolic remarks like this were an everyday occurrence when working with the witches. I often wondered what they said about me when I wasn't there. Although, if they thought that it would have bothered me, then they were mixing me up with someone who cared!

One of the posts that I covered on a regular basis was the prison laundry. The workparty consisted of around ten to fifteen female inmates and they were very efficient in the way that they processed all the prisons laundry as well as the outside contracts such as Stirling County Rugby Club strips and Stirling Albion Football strips. The machines were massive and could handle huge loads. Thousands of items per day could come through the laundry and only very rarely did even a single pair of knickers go missing. Everything was labelled and logged into the system by the hardworking women. I was surprised by how enthusiastic the prisoners were when they were working, not the preconceived idea one may have of them.

Staff were allowed to bring in duvets etc to have them laundered for a nominal fee. Occasionally I would bring in my ironing to do in my lunch break but one of the inmates would spot my polythene bag and have it done for me. As a thank you I would leave a wee treat of a cake or packet of chocolate biscuits on their table for their tea break. There were many decent women who worked in the laundry and they were in for various and sometimes, idiotic reasons. Jean told me she was in for non-payment of fines that kept multiplying exponentially and she found it impossible to pay them off. 'What were you fined for, Jean?' I asked her. I was shocked when she said that it all started off when a penalty for not having a TV licence went unpaid. It sounded incredible to me that anyone could ultimately go to prison for such a reason.

In 1995 Cornton Vale had an Open Day and the staff were allowed to bring family and friends to look around the place. My old Dad used to watch the Australian TV serial-drama 'Prisoner Cell Block H' set in a fictitious female jail and he used to ask me if the Vale was like that. I would have a laugh with him and say, 'Yes Dad, we have all the usual suspects and characters in here *and* our very own 'vinegar tits' too. The difference being, our walls don't judder like cardboard when we slam the doors!' My Dad was fascinated by it all. He especially found it hilarious when prisoners would walk past us and joke with me. He was shocked that women who knew me well called me John or in some cases, 'Crooky'. I don't know what he expected, to be honest, but I am pleased that he got the chance to look around the place and see that prisoners were ordinary people with issues just like everyone else.

At the end of a normal working day in the laundry, I would be locking the place up and notice sitting on the table waiting for me near the exit, was a couple of black bin bags. This would be my neatly folded and pressed clothes along with some delicate items on polythene-protected hangers too.

It's exceedingly remarkable what you can get in Cornton Vale for a couple of Mr Kipling Victoria sponge cakes. Other makes of sponge cake are available!

A MISTAKE WITH FUEL AND ESCORTED BY A FOOL

Sometime early in 1999, I had been scheduled to work in the newly formed Industrial Cleaning workparty. It wasn't the easiest shift to do as the women were working in nearly every area of the prison and keeping tabs on every one of them almost required you to be omnipresent, if not, omnipotent!

I had placed the women in the sections that had been programmed for cleaning and headed back to the office to catch up on the paperwork. I had been sitting for no more than five minutes when the phone rang; it was the control room supervisor.

She explained that they were extremely short staffed this morning and could I help out by driving the prison car to Forfar sheriff court via Arbroath with another officer and a prisoner.

'Back of the net!' I thought, anything to get out of here for a while. I cancelled the morning cleaning regime and arranged for the workparty to be collected and taken back to their respective blocks and headed to the gate.

The Vauxhall Cavalier two-litre diesel car was sitting waiting for me with the aforementioned twosome in the back handcuffed to each other. I drove the sixty or so miles to Arbroath where we were to take the inmate, Shiela, to a contact centre to meet her daughter. She was to have a short one-hour visit, then on to the courthouse at Forfar, a further fifteen or so miles away.

It had been an uneventful journey until we left the contact centre, and I informed the two in the back seat that we needed fuel before we started the second leg of the trip, so I pulled into a Shell filling station in Arbroath town centre and proceeded to 'fill her up!' I picked up the nozzle and began to dispense the fuel. I started daydreaming about other things and before I knew it the nozzle clicked to tell me it was full, yes full right to the brim with *unleaded* petrol, then I realised this was a *diesel* car! OOPS!

I had the foresight to realise that turning the key to start the engine would only further exacerbate my predicament, so I stuck my head into the car to let the other officer, Rosie, know what had happened.

'For fuck sake John, what are we going to do? We need to be at Forfar sheriff court for one o'clock and it's nearly quarter past twelve now!' screeched Rosie in a panicked tone.

'You'll need to phone a taxi.' I answered. 'I'll arrange to have this car emptied of petrol and refilled with diesel, I'll catch up with you at Forfar, ok?'

Their two gobs looked well and truly smacked!

Unimpressed, Rosie, with her prisoner handcuffed to her, headed into the kiosk to use their phone to call a taxi for them both, while I arranged for a local recovery firm to sort out my mess.

Twenty minutes passed, very slowly. It felt like a large crowd of onlookers had gathered to wave me off, as I sat behind the wheel in full uniform with a big red-face and looking mortified while the mechanic's large recovery truck proudly towed me out of the forecourt.

When I eventually arrived at Forfar sheriff court later that afternoon I got the impression that Rosie had told everyone what had happened. The mocking, repartee and witty banter from the cops and all the other screws from various jails, was just what I needed to wind down from that stressful morning at the petrol station!

Getting away from the prison, be it in the form of an escort or a driver, can be a welcome relief from the mundane routine. During the lockdown at Glenochil, I had been sent to Glasgow sheriff court with big Sammy the officer plumber and John Moran who was an officer joiner in the estates department and both were as daft as a brush, in a good way. This was the first time I had been on an escort and those guys kept me right.

So there we were; a painter, a plumber, and a joiner, escorting an infamous category A prisoner, who cannot be named due to the Official Secrets Act, to Glasgow sheriff court and back to Glenochil. That doesn't sound like it will end well. It didn't but not for the reasons you might expect.

The prisoner was sat in the middle seat in the back of the dark blue saloon handcuffed to big Sammy's left arm and to my right arm. John Moran was in the front with the driver P.O. Mr. Wheeler, which I thought was unusual as the gaffers are normally above driving. It was all very routine stuff on the journey and we arrived in the underground cellblock area at the court building on schedule, the police took our prisoner and kindly locked him in a cell for us. The prison staff are then free to go upstairs to the common areas and restaurants.

Woohoo breakfast!

This beats hanging around a dreary depressing jail any day of the week. In fact I was out doing escorts for weeks on end as they were so short staffed in areas around the jail and most of us estates officers had opted to work 48 hours a week and escorts could be long days. I liked escorts; they were as good as a holiday.

I remember on our way back from Glasgow to Glenochil that afternoon and the P.O. Frank Wheeler was driving again. I was in the front seat this time and for some reason he was intimidating other drivers by pulling up level with them and staring at them letting them see his epaulettes. How odd! I thought, 'This guy's a live one.' He wasn't even hiding it from us! The prisoner in the back seat noticed as well and everyone got a bit uneasy. P.O. Wheeler even said at one point, "Watch this guy shittin' it when I pull up beside him, he thinks we are the polis."

Aaarrgg!

He was the talk of the Steamie when we got back to the jail. Mr. Wheeler's given name was Frank and staff used his full name as a sort of Spoonerism and referred to him as Wank Freewheeler, which was mildly amusing, especially after his escort antics. Even the Cat A was laughing!

PROSTITUTES, NURSES AND WEE FURRY PURSES

Every jail I worked in had certain staff that were referred to as 'Ospreys' because they were seen to be a protected species. Having been chosen to work permanently in the Gatelodge, Electronic Control Room (ECR) Control and Operations Room (COR) or anywhere else that was deemed a cushy post. They guys were excused prisoners and it always seemed to be the same officers, funnily enough. I often wondered if there was an arcane reason for this, some sort of twisted nepotism maybe. I mean, like, was there a family/friends/club/lodge connection or something going on there? Probably. Those were certainly the rumours. It was often said it would be a great job if it weren't for prisoners!

At that time, I was one of only about a dozen male officers working in Cornton Vale. I suppose you could say that we were novelty value to the inmates, who had up until that time been used to dealing with only female officers. I believe female staff took a slightly firmer approach with inmates of the same gender, but female inmates at the Vale were shown, in my opinion, more patience by male officers. I can't be sure if this phenomenon works in reverse at male establishments.

The lassies, as they were referred to, would wind-up male officers using humour and sexual innuendo and their wit was as sharp as a tack. They gave nicknames to most staff and we had a 'Dulux' because his name was Matthew (Matt) White. Another was nicknamed 'Budgie' because their surname was Cheape. There was a 'Bunny' as his surname was O'Hare and we also had a 'Stella' because she was partial to the odd lager or two. I had a few shifts working with a guy who we nicknamed 'Cobweb' because he was often found hanging around in dark corners. I was only ever known as Crooky or occasionally Crooksy but I'm sure they could've been a bit more creative with that surname; maybe they did but no one ever told me! Everyone took it in a good-natured way and there was seldom any kickback.

Self-harm was the main issue at Cornton Vale and a lot of the inmates should have been anywhere else except a prison. If "Code Red" crackled over the communication panel or through your radio, you knew there was going to be blood when you got there, sometimes lots of blood. This was all depending on whether or not the poor lassie had intentionally tried to take her own life by slashing her wrists with a blade taken from a disposable razor, or if "Code Blue" was the shout then it was signalling someone who had difficulty breathing and had probably tried to hang themselves in some desperate cry for help. Most of these women were crying out for help, let down by the education, health and social care systems that had intolerantly thrown them onto the scrapheap years ago.

Epilepsy was also a major issue in a lot of jails and a fair percentage of inmates suffered from this debilitating condition. It wasn't a typical day at the Vale if staff didn't have to deal with a prisoner suffering a seizure. Stabbings and slashings were a regular occurrence too but mostly confined to male establishments; as were staff assaults, random outbreaks of fighting and lots of suicide attempts.

Sadly, during my time at Cornton Vale, three women whom I had got to know well had succeeded in taking their own lives. There had been a few suicides before I arrived in 1994 and I assume that more occurred after I had left in 2003. The womens' stories were, for me, sadder than the male inmates' stories. Yes, that might be because I'm looking at it from a male perspective; but many of them seemed to start off life within an abusive family and then moved on to develop subsequent abusive relationships throughout their adult lives. Maybe they brought out the paternal instinct in me, as a lot of the inmates were now much younger than I was, given that our ages are constantly changing. There were sixteen year olds in Cornton Vale and they acted and looked a lot younger, some were only just out of secure units. If they thought they'd learnt anything from those places, prison was going to seem like a Criminal University of New Technology. Please excuse the acronym!

The prison kitchen was an interesting place to find oneself. Well-equipped and modern, it was in total, staffed by four male catering officers at the time I worked there. For inmates, this was the highest paid job in the jail, and 'early cooks' and 'late cooks' worked two separate shifts to keep over two hundred hungry women fed, as well as the occasional baby or two! At that time inmates were able to keep their babies with them up until they reached a certain age; I think it may have been up to a year. There were special mother and baby units within the establishment. I would be surprised if this has changed.

It wasn't unusual to be walking up the path to your office in the morning and a couple of inmates were walking toward you pushing their wee babies in prams and buggies, some had even been born while their mother was serving a sentence. All the other inmates in the block made such a fuss over the babies and were just desperate to help out the mother in every way that they could. A motherly instinct is a fascinating thing to watch in such a place and it was heartening to witness their empathy, kindness and altruism; which was a stark contrast to what some of them had been convicted for.

Anyway, back to the kitchen. I loved working the odd shift in there as I was just left to get the job done without distractions. Occasionally I would get the time to make a huge pot of curry for everyone's lunch and for an hour or so it felt like I was working in a restaurant rather than such a depressing place as a prison.

Big Rhoda, a well-known recidivist, was helping me prepare the aforementioned curry one morning and we were having the usual piss taking exchange. Rhoda was telling me that she worked as a freelance escort in Kilmarnock. It paid very well she told me but the cops were always on her case giving her a hard time. I asked her if prostitution was the reason she was in prison. 'Naw, I'm in for receiving swollen goods!' she giggled. The first time I met Rhoda was in Assessment at the work allocation board where I was the job allocator.

Me: "Name?"

Her: "Rhoda."

Me: "Surname?"

Her: "Rotten"

Me; "Rhoda Rotten?"

Her: "Aye and she loved it! Ha ha ha ha ha"

Me: "Aye, very good!"

Rhoda, as it turned out, was serving a couple of years this sentence but had previously been in jail for shorter terms. She had knifed a client in a hotel room after he had refused to part with the £50.00 owed to her for 'services rendered'. There was a struggle and the guy pulled a knife on Rhoda and had tried to rob her. She told me that she had, 'Swiftly parted his balls with a size five *Jimmy Choo* stiletto.'

The pain made him drop his knife and she grabbed it. Ignoring him shouting and cursing in agony at her, she plunged it into his thigh so that he would let go of her wrist. Rhoda broke free and ran out of the room fearing for her life. Leaving the man on the floor bleeding from a cut to his leg and a lot of explaining to do, she ran out of the building into the anonymity of the streets. Rhoda admitted to being no innocent angel, but given that she'd acted in self defence and that the knife belonged to the guy; she felt that her sentence of two years wouldn't have been half that, had she been a 'Miss Normal', a cleaner, a factory worker or a cook. You can't argue with that.

'Fuckin' sheer hypocrisy!' she complained. 'It was the mere fact that I was renting out my fanny, that was my downfall!'

'Were you able to sustain a decent living from it, Rhoda?' I asked her.

'Definitely, in fact if I had another pair of legs, I would've opened a branch in Kilwinning!' she joked.

Another prisoner of note was Sonya Price. Sonya was a troubled soul who was normally only nuisance value and posed no more of a threat than a Jack Russell with a bone. This particular morning Sonya was displaying a more heated side of her personality and was smashing up her room and screaming like a Banshee for reasons unknown. Staff had been ordered to relocate her into the 'soft room' for her own protection and everyone else's safety (and sanity!) This relocation involved her being strip-searched by female staff, placed in a hospital type gown and then taken to a room with padded walls at the other end of the wing. Once the officers were satisfied that she wasn't in possession of anything that she could use to cause further damage to herself, they left her to cool down.

A few minutes later the staff were checking on her through the observation glass and there was the bold Sonya sitting squat-legged on the floor facing them, and according to one female officer in attendance,

'She had pulled a can of Fizzy Orange from her wee furry vending machine!'

She had apparently been taunting them through the observation window as she slurped from the slightly bashed can.

Sonya's nickname after that? 'Fanta Fanny!'

This was the smuggling method that a lot of inmates in Cornton Vale had favoured when trying to conceal their contraband. They called the act 'banking' the goodies and coarsely referred to their vagina as their 'wee furry-purse' and it could hold more than some loose change and a lipstick, as Sonya had just demonstrated.

Some lassies that were due for release were allowed home for weekend visits and they'd occasionally 'pack their furry purse' with as many goodies as it would hold, before returning to the jail. Some were caught at the reception because they had been too greedy and over enthusiastic when banking the loot, which caused them to walk oddly with strange stilted movements. 'You would walk oddly with strange stilted movements too if you'd packed your fanny full of trinkets and objet d'art, John!' one of the staff told me when I'd remarked on it.

Normally they would just walk straight through the security procedure without anyone raising an eyebrow. Others were caught however, with items such as miniature bottles of vodka, condoms full of Charlie, sex toys and mobile phones. Those were mighty big phones that they manufactured in the nineties and I often wondered how they had managed to conceal the colossal charger that would have been needed into such a small pouch?

I had to laugh on one occasion when a less than streetwise inmate referred to hers as, 'My wee furry duffle bag.' I don't think she fully understood her own analogy! This sort of coarse humour was commonplace at Cornton Vale.

Another crude example: I was standing on the grass next to the dog unit with two inmates from the Gardens workparty. Tim the dog handler was out exercising the Springer Spaniel, Millie. We got chatting and after a few minutes the dog was lying down at Tim's feet and had started licking herself between the legs, as dogs do.

'I wish ah could dae that!' laughs Betty, looking over at the dog.

Her pal Agnes answers, 'You'd better give her a biscuit first, she might bite ye!'

MALE ON MALE ASSAULT BUT WHO WAS AT FAULT

Sometimes the humour in jails could be more shadowy.

One bright September morning I was on duty in the gatehouse at Cornton vale. The papers had been delivered as usual and we set about organizing them into separate piles according to the prisoners' location. We didn't normally have time to scratch our arses never mind read the paper, but this particular morning I noticed a headline in a national daily redtop about a prison officer. The story described how the officer had been sexually assaulted while attending a teambuilding course at a local business hotel frequently used by the SPS, so I paused for a moment to take in the details.

I knew that a colleague, with whom I had worked at Glenochil, had recently been on a teambuilding course in the area and I was naturally curious to find out if he had been involved. Greg had attended the course along with about twenty other officers from various Scottish jails.

Reading the article further, it reported that it was a 'male on male' attack. I began to hypothesize if it may have been high-jinx that had got out of hand and ended up being unavoidably brought to the attention of management.

I had worked very closely with Greg at Glenochil and we used to mock each other all the time so I sent him an email, with badly chosen humour, asking if he was the culprit? Oh dear how inappropriate of me. I later heard from another mutual colleague and friend that it *was* actually Greg who had been the victim of the sexual assault and he was off work on sick leave suffering from stress as a result. I felt mortified about the email I had sent him so I immediately phoned him.

"Hello Greg, how are you mate? I heard you were off with stress. I feel bad now for sending you that email with our usual japes, I'm really sorry." I told him.

'I've been off for 2 weeks now John and I haven't read any emails from work.' Greg replied.

'Well, when you return to work, please ignore or delete any email you see from me, I'm so embarrassed!' I said.

Greg laughed, thankfully, before adding, 'Were you taking the piss out of me ya big shitehawk?'

'Aye I was, but I'd sent the email before I knew that it was *you* who had been assaulted Greg. I apologise to you mate, that was insensitive of me.' I told him.

'No worries, mate.' He answered.

Greg went on to tell me what had happened. He said they had all been out on moorland doing team-building exercises all day and once back at the hotel, had eaten dinner before hitting the bar. These courses were an excuse to get drunk and nearly everyone participated in this pursuit, as you can imagine. He said the rooms were like 'wee luxury cells' and there were two officers to a room, very cozy. Too cozy maybe, as Greg was awoken in the small hours with, in his own words, "A hairy-faced bastard munching on my dick!"

He told me he couldn't get the image of the other officer 'giving him a blow job', out of his head and that it was driving him crazy. I found this shocking, unbelievable almost and I told Greg I wasn't surprised that it was playing over and over in his head. I really felt for him, poor guy, that must have been very distressing. What he told me next though was incredible!

He went on, 'I was so enraged with what I was experiencing that I grabbed the guy and started punching him repeatedly in the face. He tried to get out of the room but I grabbed him and started punching him again, but he managed to flee the room. I ran out into the corridor after him and saw him enter the communal toilets. I wasn't even sure if I was dreaming or if it was or real. I followed him into the toilet area and managed to grab him again, gripping his head and pushing it against a hand-dryer machine, knocking it off the wall in the process. The next thing I knew I was being lifted off him by a group of officers who heard the noise and had came to investigate.'

I couldn't believe my ears at what I had just heard. I thought to myself that it must have been an awful experience to be assaulted in such a way by a co-worker, who only hours earlier had been exercising and socialising with you. I don't know how I would have reacted had I been the victim.

A year or so later I dropped into visit Greg in the new home he and his wife had moved to and I was keen to hear how he was doing. At first he seemed his normal cheery self and we both joked about the old days in Glenochil, but Greg's facial expression and demeanour changed when I questioned him about recent events. I thought this story couldn't get any more surreal. What I found out next is that real life is much stranger than works of the imagination!

Unknown to Greg at the time of moving into his new house; already living straight across the road from him was the guy who 'blew his job'.

Greg told me, 'The day after I moved in here, I saw him washing his car in his driveway and thought it was a hallucination!'

Like they say these days, you couldn't make this shit up and fact sure *is* stranger than fiction!

THE WEE FIFE HOUSEWIFE

A bit of respite from the usual crazy nonsense came when I was given a shift in the residential block, *Bruce House,* one morning. The workparty's were closed due to a staff shortage; when this happens they draw staff from other areas into the residential blocks and I was drafted in to assist. This wasn't part of my normal remit and being in their 'house' I felt a bit outside of my comfort zone, so to speak. I had known most of these women whilst they were at work in the gardens, sewing machines, laundry etc., but outside the work area, the change was evident.

After breakfast was over and cleaning up done, I sat chatting with a couple of familiar faces in the dining room. I barely knew their names but it was light-hearted and the time passed quicker. Andrea, whom I had spoken to several times but not at any great depth, came over to the empty chair beside me and asked if I could help her to write a letter to her daughter who was twelve.

'I don't know if I'm the right person to be doing that Andrea?' I said to her. 'Should that not be your unit or personal officer who should be doing that for you? I wouldn't want to be overstepping the mark.'

Andrea reassured me that it was ok and that she trusted me because I had helped one of her friends with a similar request while she was working in my workparty. I walked with her down the corridor to the office where she started to tell me her story of despair. She was dyslexic and only needed help with phrasing and spelling. She was a bright woman who had made a massive miscalculation of judgement and was, in her own words, 'in a desperate place right now!'

'I would be happy to help you Andrea.' I said with a smile.

It turned out that her daughter Sophie now lived with her grandparents since her conviction the year before. She told me that she and Sophie had lived with her husband Larry, in a Forestry Commission 'tied house' as a family, before their lives were torn apart by her actions following a moment of pent up rage.

Andrea and Larry had been dropping young Sophie off at a friend's house for a sleepover. She and Larry then returned to their detached property overlooking the Ballo reservoir in Fife, tranquil and very serene; the antithesis of what married life was for them at the time. Andrea said that Larry was a bully who drank all the time causing upset and massive rows in the home. It was getting worse and he had started to use his fists. Fearing for her and Sophie's wellbeing, she hatched an escape plan that had gone too far. That night, after receiving yet another reign of blows to the side of her head delivered by Larry's huge hairy fists, Andrea decided enough was enough and when he eventually collapsed in a drunken stupor on top of their bed, she gathered together the miscellaneous articles and paraphernalia needed to carry out her mission; a change of clothes, car keys, fuel, cigarettes, a lighter and some cash.

Larry had shotguns in their garage that were used for his job so Andrea helped herself to a 28" Webley & Scott twelve bore. She loaded both barrels with cartridges and calmly walked back to her kitchen and through the hallway to their bedroom where she emptied both barrels into the sleeping giant's body at almost point blank range. Larry never flinched; only the jolt from the few hundred pellets hitting his body had buzzed him like a defibrillation shock, *twice,* spraying blood up the walls and ceiling and almost severing him in two!

Andrea guessed that nobody would hear the gunshot as they were surrounded by trees and their nearest neighbours were almost a mile away, besides gunshots were an everyday occurrence in these parts so hardly a suspicious sound. They would certainly *see* the results of her next move! To cover up the shotgun incident, Andrea thought that setting fire to the house to burn all evidence was the best idea; she said that she'd once seen it on an ITV drama. The gallon can of two-stroke was doused over the bed and the surrounding floors. Once she had started the car and cleared her exit the blue touchpaper was lit; BANG, her fate was sealed!

Her alibi was that she came home to find the house on fire and her husband missing. She hadn't reckoned though on the Police and Fire investigation teams being so thorough in their examination. Unlike Andrea's hero *Hercule Poirot* whom she watched avidly on ITV, these guys had forensic DNA and specialist equipment, which revealed an accelerant had been used, namely petrol, and that the body found in the bedroom was dead before the fire had started. The pathology report stated that as there was no smoke in the victim's lungs, he wasn't breathing when the smoke filled the room. I'm guessing that the hundreds of pellets in the corpse was a dead giveaway too!

Oops Andrea, fundamental error! Set the fire first *then* fire the shot (!?) well maybe not, but nevertheless she was found guilty of murder and sentenced to Life imprisonment with a fifteen-year tariff.

It always alarmed me that people who were convicted of these crimes, claimed that *they* were the original victims who saw no other way out of their dilemma. Why not just leave *before* there's a trail of bodies? Another strange peculiarity was the number of prisoners who had found their love for 'The Lord Jesus Christ' after being locked up for a long sentence.

'God made me do it!'

'Yea right, like, God talks to idiots like you!'

RICKY ROSS AND SOME OTHER DROSS

Every prison has at least some connection to a religious group or other and Cornton Vale had many such connections. Nuns, priests, rabbis and vicars would come in and speak to the lassies, and local church fellowship groups would be in and out every week.

In my role as a member of the prisons' entertainment committee, I got to know a very pleasant wee fella called Bill McGibbon. He was from one such Christian Fellowship group and he was extremely well connected. He phoned me one morning to ask if he could bring a popular artist in to play a gig. I wondered who this 'artist' could be?

Turned out to be none other than Dame Evelyn Glennie the award-winning percussionist! Wow! Who else did Bill have up his sleeve, I wondered? Evelyn played a full hour and 15 minute set to a stunned gym hall full of staff and inmates and what a charming lady she was. So flawless was her act and her banter between songs, that the inmates were unaware of the fact that Evelyn was profoundly deaf until she disclosed it to make her particular narrative at the time more amusing. Evelyn Glennie was a wonderful personality and a gorgeous woman.

Bill's second offering was Alistair Macdonald the Scottish folk singer. The inmates were a bit bemused at first and failed to find the humour in Alistair's act so he just beat them over the head with it until they did; and funnily enough it worked! By the end of the afternoon they were singing along and taking part in childish singing games with him, which involved songs with words like,

'I'M A CAT, I'M A CAT, I'M A GLESGA CAT AND MY NAME IS SAM THE SKULL

I'VE GOT CLAWS ON MY PAWS LIKE A CROCODILE'S JAWS AND A HEID LIKE A FERMERS BULL

I'M NO' THE KIND OF CAT THAT SAT ON A MAT OR THE KIND THAT YE GI' A HUG

I'M THE KIND OF CAT THAT STRANGLES RATS AND EVEN THE OCCASIONAL DUG!'

The last image I have of that mad day is a long chain of inmates holding on to each other's waist, doing congas around the hall. Alistair was clicking his heels at the front, leading the way with guitar in hand, highly amusing to watch.

Many other decent acts came and went over the years but the most exciting for me was Ricky Ross from Deacon Blue. My lead guitarist friend Neil Turner and myself greeted Ricky at the gate and after a quick sound check, took him for lunch to the staff restaurant. He was such a pleasant guy and very chatty and sociable. He even told us a story about a squirrel that came to their garden in Glasgow each day, and that he and his wife Lorraine and their children hand fed it.

I asked Neil to play a 20-minute warm up set with me before Ricky came on. There we were, playing our acoustic guitars and singing to Ricky Ross who was seated right in the middle of all the prisoners listening and applauding us, very bizarre but exciting all the same. We played about half a dozen songs before the main event, which was more than plenty. I had borrowed a top of the range electric piano from my mate Andy Simpson who owned the Keyboard Centre in Stirling's Old Arcade. Full size and full sound. Thank you Andy.

Ricky Ross was an awesome act to watch and at such close quarters too, only inches away from my eyes and ears. I could hear his every breath as he effortlessly flitted from piano to acoustic guitar. He rattled through all the hits with ease, 'Dignity' – 'Real Gone Kid' – 'Chocolate Girl' – 'Loaded' – 'When Will You Make My Phone Ring' etc. The prisoners were spellbound and so were all the screws that were seated and standing around the walls of the hall. His wee stories that he shared between songs were endearing him to the crowd and they sat in complete silence, hanging on his every word. It was only when a sing-a-long chorus bit was played that they couldn't help themselves any longer and drowned him out with their warbling.

He told them he felt like he was on 'Stars In Their Eyes' because every time he started a song and the inmates recognised it, they would start cheering and applauding, Las Vegas style. The next time it happened everyone started laughing, it was self evidently very funny.

Ricky thanked Neil and myself for our contribution and after receiving a huge bunch of flowers and a kiss from a notorious Scottish villain, he was off back to celebrity land to count his squirrels. An amazing day!

As it turns out, that wasn't the only time I got to sing for the prisoners at Cornton Vale. I was the singer in a band along with old veteran Neil Turner once again, a year or two later and we were invited in to do a set. 'Apex' had a lot of gear; drums, keyboards, guitars, lights, smoke machine, the lot. My other mate 'Ziggy' was on the lights and sound mixing desk and was like a dog with two tails; getting loads of attention from the female inmates as he sat rooted right in the centre of them all! The prisoners loved it and were standing up on their chairs dancing and singing along. The staff became agitated by this and were running around the gym telling prisoners not to stand on the seats. At the same time I was encouraging them to dance and the officers and myself had a good-humoured battle of wits going for a while. It was futile, the only way they were going to sit down was if we stopped playing and that wasn't going to happen either! All I could see was a huge dark gymnasium with a wall of prisoners' faces and the occasional white shirted screw bobbing along just like the rest!

That conjures up an image of a previous gig I played at Rosyth Naval Base and the Mess room we were set up in was next to the guardroom at the main East gate. We were rocking our socks off when I glanced out the side door to see the two sailors on guard duty with sub-machine guns held up against their chests, rocking back and forth in time to our rendition of the R.E.M. song 'It's The End Of The World As We Know It!'

Very amusing!

IT'S AN INSIDE JOB BY CROOK AND ROBB!

I was on an overnight trip to Full Sutton prison near York with two older female officers called Irene and Anne. While we were there one of our tasks was to deliver goods that had been made at Cornton Vale, to a charity shop in the Shambles area of York.

Sleeping overnight at a hotel on the outskirts of the town, I was awoken by the telephone next to my bed ringing at 7am. It was Irene to tell me that our hire car had been broken into in the hotel's car park. The rear window of the estate car had been smashed and the load cover ripped off. Most of the duvet sets, knitted toys and fancy crafts had been removed. I had to phone the police for a crime number to have the rear glass replaced by the insurance:

'Hello we're a group of prison officers from Scotland. We're down visiting the area and are calling in to Full Sutton Prison this afternoon and our vehicle has been broken into overnight in our hotel's car park.' Says me.

The cop on the other end of the phone enquires,

'You're a group of Scottish prison officers you say? What are your names and what hotel are you staying at?' in his broad Yorkshire accent.

'We are in The Grange Hotel on the Clifton Road', I answer, before adding, '...and our names are Irene Robb and John Crook.'

The silence was deafening. I could almost see his face change expression; he must've looked as puzzled as a Spaniel that had just been shown a magic trick.

'Is this a fuckin' wind up sir?' asks the cop. 'No, why?' I reply.

'Well, you say that you are a group of Scottish prison officers with names Crook and Robb and that you want to report a car burglary?' he answers.

'Aye!' says me, laughing like a bloody hyena cause I knew that I wasn't winding him up, but as far as wind-ups go this one was perfect because it was true. When we eventually arrived at Full Sutton prison that afternoon the staff already knew all about our dilemma as the police had called them to verify our story!

Names have always amused and intrigued me and I have met and worked alongside many people over the years with odd sounding, if not hilariously apt ones.

Mary-Jane Toker was probably the best name ever and if you don't get it, ask one of your cannabis-smoking friends; and if you don't know anyone who smokes cannabis, all I can say is, my what a blissfully sheltered life you must live. Either that or your friends are good liars?

Rab Findlay worked in Barlinnie with me and was transferred into The Vale around 1995. He earned the nickname, Myra, because his surname rhymed with Hindley. Rab was likeable enough but for a manager, as sheepish as a lamb, almost as much of a doofus as Murdo Fraser MSP.

I remember an older civilian lady who had recently started working in the admin block, telling us that she had been 'telling all her pal's down the bingo' that the actual Myra Hindley was being held at Cornton Vale, all because she used to hear us talking about 'Myra' every day!

I used to hang around in my early twenties with a guy called Hugh Rae. If I had been a bit more quick-witted in those days, I would've nicknamed him 'Hip-Hip'!

I used to stop on my way to work for a newspaper in the days when they still printed stuff that was worth reading and the Asian fella who ran the store was called Ahmed Adoudu.

One of my old workmates got the brilliant nickname 'Heid First' because his name was R. Slater, and I actually worked with a guy named Mike Hunt from Airdrie while I was serving my decorating apprenticeship.

I remember one day my old Dad visited me at my house and two of my mates from Cornton Vale were there with me. Their names were Justin and Jerome but just trying to stop my Dad calling them 'Robson and Jerome' was priceless!

We had a friend and neighbour in the housing scheme where I grew up, called Willie Dick. And no he wasn't, actually he was a very charming and pleasant man!

And finally, there was a girl in my cousin's class from the United States and her name made her sound like she had a

lisp. Her name was Thelma Thoale. Oh and wait for it ... she came from a family who were all devout Christians.

Like I keep saying, you couldn't make this up!

SET ME LOOSE FROM THIS MADHOOSE

Some unscrupulous male staff loved working with females and their behaviour was sometimes on the wrong side of what was morally acceptable. So much so that several had found themselves with more than just a red face.

One unfortunate officer in particular fell head over heels in love with Veronica, a very pretty woman in her late forties from Dumfries who, at the time, was serving only a few months for a vice-related crime. She had been in and out of 'The Vale' most of her adult life and was on first name terms with a lot of the staff. This mattered not a jot to our protagonist, Sam, as he secretly arranged to meet up with Veronica on her release.

Sam had already accepted an early retirement package from the SPS and the last we heard they'd got engaged and had set up home together. Once outside the confinement of prison life their relationship apparently bloomed, blossomed and then withered like a dried dandelion. It lasted no more than the time it took for her to lure Sam into a false sense of security. He was so gullible that he'd opened a joint bank account for them, where all their money was deposited and allowed her control over all their finances. After getting her hands on his lump sum payment she dumped him and fled their love-nest, disappearing off the face of the earth. Veronica had played the long game, a sorry lesson indeed for poor Sam.

Drew, an estates officer, was hornier than a three-peckered pot-belly and very partial to the smile of a damsel in distress too. He and his passwoman were caught by a social worker in a stationery room, where it's alleged that young Drew had her over a table and was, 'Riding her like Lester Piggot on Derby Day'! It's rumoured that he had his uniform trousers around his ankles and his big white space hopper bobbing up and down like the harvest moon. The social worker, Sharon, had apparently gone into the locked and seldom used stationery room to pick up some A4 paper for the photocopier and had stumbled across the startled pair of randy romancers. Rubbing her eyes in disbelief like a cartoon character, she fled the scene back to her office.

'What's the matter Sharon?' her colleague asks.

'I think I've just seen big Drew the joiner shaggin' his passwoman in our stationery room!' exclaims the red-faced Sharon.

By the time the two social workers had returned to confront them, Drew and his passwoman had not surprisingly, vanished. The incident was reported to the Governor and an in-house investigation was carried out but apparently there was no case to answer because the prisoner had denied it had ever happened. It was the two social workers' word against Drew and his tight-lipped prisoner. The case was dismissed due to insufficient evidence. Drew's punishment? He was immediately transferred 'under a cloud' to Low Moss, a male establishment near Glasgow. Hardly a punishment as he lived in Bishopbriggs and it had cut his daily commute by over an hour. I often wondered if Drew developed any passionate relationships with any of his passmen at HMP Low Moss!

Staff transfers were a regular and necessary occurrence in most prisons and one promotion into The Vale in particular was to change my working life in the SPS, significantly.

Joe Kerr was originally from Sanquhar (rhymes with banker) and was transferred in as a line manager. My big pal Phil said he had worked with him for a year or two in Greenock and told me he was, 'About as much use as tits to a Billy goat.' Joe Kerr was part of the Regimes group but not originally on my division but he was soon manipulating the rotas and rosters so that he could bully, harass and generally intimidate certain members of staff that he felt weren't conforming to his utopian vision for the Regimes group, of which I was a part. I cannot abide bullies and I let him know this by my non-compliance to his proposed changes and treated him with the apathy and disdain that he and his kind always deserve. Even the inmates hated 'Wang' Kerr because of the way he spoke to them.

Davy Nichols had been my line manager for nearly five years and we'd never had a cross word between us, ours was a relationship of trust and quid pro quo. I naively thought that it would always be this way, and then Joe Kerr arrives to spoil our cozy wee situation. Big Phil joked that it was, '…all aboard the 'Wanker from Sanquhar' Express for a trip to fucking nowhere!'

I am aware of the concept, new broom sweeps clean and all that, but Kerr was so new in his roll that you could still smell the bullshit emanating from his overly inflated sense of self. I guess what I'm trying to say is that I ended up detesting this sycophantic wee runt with such a passion; he was so far up the number one Governor's jacksey, that you could just make out his toes disappearing into the distance. He seemed to be on my case and in my face at every opportunity and I would bite like a tormented salmon every time. On one such occasion he pushed me too far and I was called into his office for a meeting with him.

'Hi John, come in and have a wee seat,' says Kerr. 'I have called you in today just to touch base with you.'

Argh!

Even his use of that clichéd buzzword language that a lot of insecure manager types are so guilty of over-using these days, really annoyed the bejeezus out of me. 'Bullshit-bingo' the staff called it. I guess by this time, even the sound of Joe Kerr breathing in and out would sicken my mince.

I remained silent as I sat down and just let him ramble on. He was all like, 'blue-sky thinking' and let's 'square the circle' by 'thinking outside the box' you know, the usual superfluous nonsense? I still sat there saying nothing.

'Is there anything you would like to ask *me,* John?' he enquired.

I felt like saying, 'Aye, how in Christ almighty's name did you manage tae get yersel promoted, Wang?'

Instead I just shamelessly shook my head and pulled my best apathetic face, my lips remained shut. From what I could determine from the meeting, the restructuring meant that Davy would no longer be my supervisor and I was to be put into Joe Kerr's group permanently; and with immediate effect.

This displeased me greatly, as you would no doubt imagine. Tensions between Kerr and me had been building for months. I asked Davy why he was no longer my line manager. He told me that he didn't want me to be transferred but Joe Kerr insisted that I was one of the half dozen or so that were to be moved into his group. It was the final straw in a long line of straws that eventually broke the camel's back, so I snapped and called in sick the following day. If, for no other reason than to throw Kerr's plans and rotas into chaos. I would say it was the straw that broke the back of the Bactrian; as he had given me the hump more than once ... Boom!

I raised a staff grievance against him for bullying and harassment and was telephoned the following morning by the Human Resources manager, a guy who had previously worked for 20 years in Woolworths. 'This is a very serious accusation you've made against a senior member of staff John, do you realise this?' asked Mr Pick n Mix.

'What's your point caller?' I answered impudently, trying to provoke a reaction from him.

'I am calling to make you aware of the gravity of the situation and to ascertain whether or not you still want this report to be submitted, Mr Crook.' He answered.

'Do you really think a wee attempt at intimidation by you on the telephone will make me change my mind? Of course I want it to be submitted!' I answered; raising my voice just enough to ensure that my stern demeanour was understood and he backed off.

I remained on sick leave for months while the investigative process was carried out. The issue was subsequently investigated thoroughly, or so they said; but the result was, surprise surprise, inconclusive. No case to answer was the term they used, as is normally the outcome in these situations. I have no doubt as to the reason for the outcome; it was a manager of the same grade as Joe Kerr who carried out the investigation. I later heard from a colleague that his golfing chum was the investigating officer and the jungle drums seemed to paradiddle that; they certainly both seemed to know each other pretty well.

I was however transferred back onto Davy Nichols' team in my absence. Davy came out to visit me at home as my new line manager once again and informed me that if I came back to work, I would notice a lot of changes that had been put in place. A new shift pattern had been introduced and Davy sold it to me like the expert socialite he was; and still is, according to old colleagues.

Back at The Vale, I made a serious effort to re-introduce myself back into some kind of work ethic once again and to at least pretend I was still interested in remaining a 'soldier of the state'. It wouldn't last long though as the SPS like most public sector organisations at that time, was going through huge political and social-economic changes; as for me, I couldn't keep my big mouth shut and was continually locking horns with management over their petty and needless regime changes. I had become a 'rebel without a clue' and was bitter at the direction in which my career had been steered, nay, catapulted. I was desperate for an exit package and was already trying to develop strategies and running through wee hypothetical scenarios in my head, as to how this could be achieved.

NO AFFECTION IN THE PROTECTION SECTION

I first encountered Linda in the textile workshop where she was working on the cutting table marking out components for jeans. A stack of fifty layers of denim material were laid out on the giant table and Linda drew around a cardboard template with tailors chalk before using a specialist cutting machine that cut right through the fifty layers at the same time. She had worked up quite a speed at this since I'd only just shown her the task a couple of days earlier, and it quickly became apparent that she was a lot more intelligent than she was letting on to the rest of her peers.

The women in the workparty were aware that she had been sentenced to Life a few short weeks earlier for the murder of an elderly woman, but were speculative about the details. This sort of crime against vulnerable seniors does not go unnoticed by other inmates and in Linda's case this was no exception. They would taunt her at every opportunity about being a 'granny-basher' and made her already stressful life a whole lot more traumatic. Linda had been heard saying that it was her co-accused who had coerced and manipulated her into carrying out the killings.

'She's a cocky bastard, there's no way any cunt could control her!' exclaimed *Mrs Big*.

In every prison there appeared to be some bizarre moral hierarchy as to which crimes were acceptable and which one's weren't. Murder *is* acceptable but only up to the point of who is actually carrying out the killing. If you're not a typical hard-faced MURDERER with mean-street attitude, prepare to be scrutinised like an amoeba in a glass of pond water!

When I worked at Barlinnie, I remembered there being several 'protection inmates' who would be segregated from the mainstream prison population for their own personal safety. If they felt vulnerable they could ask for protection, and they would be moved to a separate accommodation block and workparty. Keeping 'protections' completely segregated and safe, as regards their working situations, posed many problems for staff and the prison eventually had so many protections that they had to open a dedicated workparty for them all. This workparty was nicknamed the 'Stoats', so called because of the old Glasgow colloquialism for sex offender, 'a stoat the ball'.

As there was no such thing, technically, as 'protection' at Cornton Vale, staff had to use their own initiative and identify vulnerable inmates who may have been getting bullied or harassed by stronger and more confident inmates.

I remember a P.E. instructor having an exchange with one of those inmates when he pulled her up for giving Linda a hard time in the gym. 'She's a fuckin' beast, Stevie, she murdered an old pensioner!' the girl snarled at him.

'I'm not here to decide which one of you are more worthy of my respect and which one isn't,' the PE instructor reminded her, before adding, 'You are each entitled to the same protection from bullying. You are all the same to me, you're all prisoners!'

This must've upset her a tad as she then started screaming, 'Are you saying that *I'm* as bad as that fucking beast?? I'm only in here for supplying drugs!'

'I know that, but if you had any humility yourself, then you would realise that *your* crime isn't a victimless one either, is it?' the instructor retorted, before adding, 'Your victims are mostly vulnerable teenagers, so don't get all sanctimonious with me about who has the moral high ground here.'

She looked at him like a petulant child who had just been grounded for a week with immediate cessation of chocolate rations! Bullying is a serious issue in prisons and although there are strategies to deal with it, it's still an everyday occurrence.

Linda had been in a relationship with her co-accused, and was captivated by his charisma and looks. Other inmates dismissed her claims that he controlled and manipulated her as pure fabrication and they saw this as her excuse to deflect any vitriol levelled against her.

Over a period of a few months, Linda and her co-accused had been watching the old couple, building up a picture of their routine. They had always been resourceful throughout their 40-year marriage and owned a lucrative amusement arcade in Portobello, Edinburgh.

The keys for the arcade were taken home every night by the elderly couple so with the abandonment of any logic, forethought or empathy they forced their way into the luxury bungalow, pushing the frail 75 year- old man against the stairs as they barged their way in. His frail wife started screaming, obviously concerned for her husband, so to shut her up a cricket bat was rattled off her left temple; she died almost instantly.

The old fella, who had been an amateur boxer in his younger days, got up and tried to defend his wife and family home but the pair were just too strong for him and he was seriously assaulted in the same manner as his wife. A cowardly and wicked act, and one for which Linda paid a heavy price. Some of the inmates ridiculed her, mostly behind her back because Linda's self-assured and confident attitude meant that it was only a tiny minority who said a word against her. She eventually became a socially accepted inmate and a case in point of that strange moral hierarchy I mentioned previously. Linda went on to work in the hairdresser's vocational training workshop, where she earned qualifications in cutting and colouring hair. She was popular with visitors to Cornton Vale and was on friendly first name terms with a group of local senior citizens who came in every Tuesday as human guinea pigs; this was a great opportunity for the workshop and the girls got to practice their 'blue rinse' skills on them in exchange for a for a free hairdo.

Her respite was short-lived however, when the press got wind of this and had printed some melodramatic story with a headline amounting to, 'Granny Killer In Cornton Pensioners Scandal'. They printed other vitriolic shite about her 'wielding' scissors inches from their heads. True, but totally taken out of context. It was ironic though, coz the old dears hadn't a clue what Linda was in jail for and actually liked her. I had to laugh though as they used to all chat away to her like, 'Linda this and Linda that, aw she's so great!'

I often wondered how quickly they would have changed their opinion had they known what she'd done?

The parole board decided that Linda had paid her debt to society and she was released on *life licence* after serving almost 14 years. However, she may be recalled to prison immediately, and without trial, if any of the conditions of her licence are broken.

I have met Linda in town a few times since her release as she now works locally as a manager with a large multinational company; and has completely turned her life around, as well as turning her back on crime. I had worked with offenders for nearly two decades and I would've been gobsmacked had Linda offended again. She is one of Cornton Vale's more positive outcomes and quite possibly one of the finest examples of rehabilitation in action. Dare I even suggest it, a success story, for once!

Another similar but different case was Angela, let's say her surname was Ferguson, from Paisley. She, like Linda, had also been sentenced to Life for murder, this time it was her husband that she had killed. Graham had been abusive towards Angela and she finally snapped after putting up with it for decades. She told me he used to come home and slap her and the kids around, demand this and that, smash up the house, the usual MO of an abusive arsehole.

She stabbed him through the torso somewhere, I can't remember exactly, it isn't important. What is important however is that Angela felt she had no other way out of her situation but to kill Graham. Is it a shocking indictment on society that a woman felt the only way out of her abusive relationship was to kill her husband?

Many will say, "She could have just left him and took the kids."

Yes, that is true, but many vulnerable women don't have anywhere to go, have no support, and feel that they won't be believed. Especially when that is exactly the rhetoric he has been brainwashing her with for years as he rained his torrent of punches down on her head while the weans either looked on in abject terror, or they were underneath her being protected by her body!

I looked at Angela as she sat across from me at her sewing machine in the Assessment workshop. She was always on edge and would jump at the least wee sound; mind you I would too if I had just been sentenced to life the previous month for murdering my partner. She seemed to be taking it rather well, maybe she reconciled it in her head as, '…at least the weans and I won't ever have to be beaten up by him again.'

I felt sorry for her; she was a poor soul. She was a quietly spoken woman and looked just like anyone who would serve you in a pub, take your pulse at a health centre or drive your local bus. She developed a sense of black humour as time went on though, which I found sinister but funny.

We were sitting in the workshop one afternoon when the door suddenly blew open for no apparent reason. Angela, quick as a flash pipes up with a giggle, "That will be Graham, letting me know he's still around watching me."

A QUANDARY IN THE LAUNDRY

I was back in the laundry for a week covering for Sheila
Taylor who was off on leave. 'Great!' I thought, 'I'll get
all that washing done that's been piling up in the Ali Baba
basket in my bathroom!'

Everything was progressing swimmingly as per usual, the
lassies had their noses to the grind and clean towels and
prisoners' personal laundry bags were flying out the door
at record speed. We were well ahead of schedule and I had
been out on the floor most of the morning helping to fold,
pack and process. I headed back into the office area to
answer the phone, it was Joe Kerr. He informs me that
before she went off on leave, him and Sheila had made a
few changes to the daily regime in the laundry. One of the
changes being, that letting the girls into the office
unattended wasn't a clever idea so it was to stop with
immediate effect. Joe Kerr told me that I'd to inform the
workparty right away, so that when Sheila returned to
work, the prisoners were already conditioned to it.

'Suits me!' I thought.

'Right ladies, before you go, I want to speak to you. Let's
have you over here for a few seconds please!' I said with
some fake gravitas, I say fake gravitas because by this time
I had been prescribed diazepam and had taken a few that
morning just to get through.

I explained to the inmates that Mr Kerr had been on the phone and that he and Mrs Taylor were concerned about the security issues of letting anyone just wander into the office, willy or indeed nilly, and as staff had personal property in there such as handbags/holdalls and suchlike, from now on anyone entering the office had to clear it with the laundry officer first. The prisoners nodded their agreement and went back to their residential units for lunch.

Phew! Sorted.

1pm arrived and the afternoon shift began to filter into the laundry. I noticed that two of the girls who were not at work in the morning had entered the workparty, so I called them both over to explain the position that I had outlined to the other ladies earlier. A local woman, Sally, whose brain was full of bees, didn't take it too well and was screaming at me, 'Are you calling me a thief??'

Sally was about 4'11" and quite podgy in the midsection.

She had her hair scraped back from her forehead in a 'junky bun' and she reminded me of Vicky Pollard from the Little Britain show.

'No Sally, why are you saying that?' I went on, trying to explain that everyone was under the same restrictions and it wasn't just her.

'Ah'll get you slashed ya big baldy cunt! I see you and yer wife and weans up the toon, so you'd better watch yersel!' she bellowed at me, among other variations of the same threat!

I had shaved my hair really short, skinhead style, as was the fashion at the time so I just laughed off the 'baldy' remark. I was more concerned with her threats towards my wife and children. I knew that she was all mouth and baggy trousers but I wanted her out of my face, so I phoned over to her unit and asked for someone to come and escort her from the workshop back to her room. I wasn't going to stand for her intimidation or threats, even if I'd believed them to be only idle ones.

It was a complete over reaction on wee Sally's part but I suspect that she was more than likely out of her face on a similar medication to the ones that I had just taken; only Sally's reaction wasn't as spectacular as what my reaction would be. Read on ...

The unit duly sent Aileen Orr, to escort wee Sally back to her room, who was still in my face screaming obscenities at me. Aileen was a veteran officer with decades of knowledge and a black belt in 'tongue' fu!

'Don't touch me, ya fat cow!' she bellowed at Aileen because she'd dared to touch her shoulder whilst escorting her out of the laundry.

'Look at you! You'll be left on the shelf 'til you die, ya ugly basturt!' she rasped at poor Aileen.

The officer answers her in a heartbeat, 'I don't mind being left on the shelf hen, as long as I'm taken down and dusted every so often!'

Brilliant!

Some prison officers are so patient under the most abrasive of circumstances. I love them *and* their inappropriate humour; they are some of the funniest people on the planet sometimes. Aileen Orr had the best retort ever!

Although this next one comes pretty close too.

Carol Maltman, the officer in charge of a new workparty had been showing a group of delegates from the home office around her new workshop studio. She was showing them some of the artworks which had been painted by the inmates. Carol had framed prints of famous paintings on the wall too. One of the delegates who was obviously quite taken by a framed picture and thinking that one of the talented female inmates was responsible, pipes up, 'Who's magnificent work is this Mrs Maltman?'

Carol looks up at the painting and tells him, "That was Claude Monet!"

My patience with the job was now beginning to wear very thin. I had been pretty impulsive throughout my career but what I did next was probably the most impulsive and irresponsible decision I had made since starting with the SPS almost eighteen years earlier. It may have been the way I felt under the influence of the diazepam I had swallowed that morning, but I just saw everything so much clearer and knew that I shouldn't be there. It was as if a switch had been pulled in my head as I immediately grabbed my jacket and bag, locked the office and walked towards the exterior door of the laundry and out into the corridor. I locked the main door of the laundry behind me, leaving around fifteen inmates inside and walked across the small courtyard leading to where the kitchen was located. My boss Davy, whose office was based in the kitchen, would want to know why I had left the laundry unattended so I went in to let him know what my intentions were!

'Hi John, you okay mate?' he enquired, suddenly realising by the expression on my face that, NO I wasn't, O-*bloody*-Kay!

'I'm going home Davy and I won't be back this time, I'm sorry.'

'EH? What's up John? Where are your prisoners?'

'They're locked in next door Davy, here's the keys!' I said as I chucked the bunch of laundry machine keys onto his desk.

'For fuck's sake John, you know better than anyone that you just can't lock them in there on their own.' He answered.

'That's not my problem any longer, Davy!' I said, as I walked out of the kitchen and headed down the path toward the main gatehouse; with Davy running after me like any anxious and concerned manager might do, especially if they were going to be left with well over a dozen extra prisoners to find cover for. By this time, I really wasn't caring any longer. The officer at the gate looked a bit taken aback when he saw me at the glass window waiting for him to unlock the electronic door. He jokingly said something to me about leaving early but I was too numb to explain it to him so I just smiled at him and said,

'See ya, widnae want tae be ya!'

I felt an exhilarated rush of adrenaline and dopamine wash over me on the way home as I realised I wouldn't be back this time! The occasional inmate had threatened me in the past but this was nothing more than posturing on wee daft Sally's part. She just happened to be in the wrong place at the wrong time and had made the mistake of screaming threats to the wrong person at the wrong time. She was a catalyst that I utilised with maximum effect.

My doctor diagnosed 'stress and anxiety' and signed me unfit for work indefinitely. It was not until around eighteen months later that I was officially 'let go' by the SPS. Not exactly the most glorious of endings to an illustrious career, but there you go.

I set foot in Cornton Vale again only once and it was to meet with the new governor, with whom I hadn't been previously familiar. Mrs Parker had taken over the reigns from her predecessor Kathy Davison while I had been off on sick leave. She thanked me for my contribution to the service over the years and said she was disappointed that we never got the opportunity to work together. It was all very cordial and business like and that suited me just fine. Besides, *her* idea of us working together and *my* idea of us working together would have been two completely different sit-coms! My last three years in the SPS were almost unbearable and I would put that down to my plummeting tolerance levels pitted against the overwhelming change in attitude by senior management and ultimately the SPS HQ.

Their, 'we care about our staff' rhetoric was hollow in my opinion. I felt that they only paid lip service to the word 'care'. Big Phil and I were talking about this and he said it was all just smoke and mirrors in an attempt to disguise the fact that you were going to be, 'Shafted so far up the arse, that you'd have two Adam's apples!' He had a way with words had our Phil. He said their objective was, '…that you would get so sick of all the unnecessary changes, you would leave the job of your own freewill and they wouldn't have to pay you any severance.' I feel that he may have had a point!

The 'Investors In People' award that big Kathy the previous Governor just loved to promote, was a symbolic joke. The only people that the SPS were investing in were the Joe Kerrs of this world closely followed by his hard-hearted and selfish clique, all in an attempt to shave a few brass farthings off the annual budget. Ordinary basic grade prison staff were always the last consideration.

All types of new management styles were being introduced to prisons all over Scotland, in the shape of ex 'captains of industry' from Burger King and Mcdonald's to Marks and Spencer and RBS.

Big Phil: "These absolute shit-for-brains wannabe high-flyers are being parachuted into senior Governors' posts that were normally only reserved for long-serving prison staff who had worked their way through the ranks and had experienced the real 'joys' of working in noxious environments like jails. Mr Merchant Banker et al hadn't a clue how to manage a prison, but he'd happily take a huge salary for trying to show more experienced 'investors' how to suck eggs!"

I hadn't a clue what Phil was talking about but it sounded good. Plus he was kind of right. There were one or two exceptions to this rule however. One woman in particular, named Alice Younger, was a remarkable 'direct entrant' into the governor grade and she angered some staff when she made a few changes that ruffled their fascist feathers.

In the reception area where inmates are processed, staff had colloquially termed the changing cubicles 'dug boxes' which, when you think about it is a pretty derogatory term, especially when you're dealing with vulnerable women. Alice made a directive that they were to be referred to as, quite rightly, changing cubicles or just cubicles. Her name and reputation became mud and a lot of the right-leaning staff took an instant dislike to her because of this. I felt however, that Alice was a much-needed breath of fresh air to Cornton Vale that had been under the direction of big Kathy Davison for far too long and was getting a bit 'Shawshanky'!

Big Kathy, in my opinion, was a shameless self-promoter and was only interested in change if it made her look good or won her accolades and glittery awards! Most decent staff faced a tsunami of shite everyday but her personal goal of making Cornton Vale a *'Centre of Excellence'* was the only target on big Kathy's agenda. Meanwhile, everyone else in the place was treading water with lead boots on! As one would imagine, this had a dramatic effect on staff morale and lots of them had fallen on their swords. It was a bit like 'boiling a frog', if you're familiar with that old analogy? It hypothesises that if you place a frog into a pan of cold water and slowly bring it to the boil, the frog won't realise it's being boiled until it's too late to do anything about it. I was one of those frogs, and I had been slowly brought to the boil and simmered for over eighteen years before I eventually croaked!

New rules and directives from the upper echelons of power would be introduced and forced on us minions at the coalface who would just have to either keep digging or leave. Before you knew it life had become so intolerable that one didn't know what to do about it. Put up or shut up I would guess; a kind of totalitarian tiptoe. It felt like they had bound our wrists and ankles with duct tape, blindfolded our eyes and stuffed a snooker ball into our mouths; then sent us in to work with hundreds of potentially dangerous people, several of whom were so dangerous they'd happily torture you if given half the chance. This would be bad enough, but if, like me, you felt that that senior management were doing little to support you or more accurately, didn't feel any desire to, then it's a hundred times worse. Box ticking seemed to be their primary objective. Like I said, lip service would be paid to their duty of care towards you, my own case being a prime example.

Davy my line manager was ordered to make a home visit to me as part of his absence management procedure and he brought Donald Milne the Human Resources boss with him. Donald was an ex Woolworth's manager who the screws at The Vale delighted in nicknaming 'Mr Pick n Mix'. He was a complete waste of oxygen and was educated way beyond his intellect.

They both arrived at our door and my wife Alicia politely took their jackets and offered them tea, all very civilised, for now. I deliberately hadn't shaved for over a week just to create that extra 'crazed madman' persona. I looked like the Wild Man of Borneo as I sat there trying to look like a broken man in my old tatty pyjamas with a ripped dressing gown over them. It was 2pm and I was drinking gin and tonics like prohibition was on the way!

Donald spouted the usual departmental line and tried his best to take the lead whilst speaking to me in his usual condescending manner. He said something to me about how relaxed it must've been to work in the regimes group and that it couldn't possibly be that stressful, given that the prisoners were all well behaved in the workshops.

'Is that right mate?' I thought. Here we go, if Don wants some Crooky in his face, then I'm going to oblige him!

'And how would you know that, Don? When was the last time you even *saw* a prisoner, unless it was the governor's passwoman bringing you a cup of tea in her frilly apron? Don't come in here and tell me where my stress comes from. You do realise your patronising attitude is why nobody in Cornton Vale has a pleasant word to say about you, don't you? No? I didn't think so. When are you going to do the decent thing, Don, and get out of my house?' I growled at him, with 18 years of pent up rage eventually manifesting itself in my outburst!

He looked shaken by my tirade of abuse as he sat there on the sofa. I could see him uncomfortably shifting from one buttock to the other as I noticed Davy out of the corner of my eye desperately trying to stifle a laugh. I don't think he was used to anyone speaking to him like that and I normally wouldn't have either but I knew I would never be going back there so I'd nothing to lose but my self-respect and ensuing exit package.

Donald Milne had been a bit of a bully to a lot of my colleagues previously so I didn't feel remorseful in the slightest. He took the overly emphasised hint and got to his feet. He thanked my wife Alicia for the tea and walked towards the door, not before asking her who had decorated our staircase, as '…it was beautiful' he said.

'Are you having a laugh Donald?' I asked rhetorically, before pointing at the front door and motioning him to exit, pronto style! What an inappropriate question, I thought. Was he serious or was he just trying to get a further rise out of me on his way out as a parting shot across the bows? It was almost as offensive to me as the phrase, "I don't like music!"

As they both walked towards the jail car, Davy glanced at me through the window, clenching his front teeth and pursing his lips to stop himself from guffawing, he got into the passenger seat and the car quickly sped off with Donald at the wheel.

I had been off sick for almost two years before I was finally free of the pedantic drivel I'd experienced at the hands of certain SPS managers, and only then because I'd insisted I wasn't making a return to work anytime soon. My nerves were shattered by the actual thought of it.

'We need your doctor to provide us with a 'window' of when you'll be returning to work Mr Crook, can you get him to do this for us?' they would ask me at every opportunity. A window? It would have to be a greenhouse as he can see you lot coming a mile off, I thought. There it is again, that management speak, a window? Why couldn't they just speak in plain language and ask when I'd be coming back to my work? It was such a contradiction to me, as at that time they had also introduced an initiative on communicating in 'plain language', where the staff were encouraged to write reports etc., in easily understood 'dumbed-down' sentences.

This irony was utterly squandered on Joe Kerr and his crew!

HERE COMES MY FUTURE FOR ALICIA TO BUTCHER

The life I had made for myself post SPS bore no resemblance to the life sentence that I had served in jail. In the short few years after leaving the prison service I had married the perfect wife, purchased the perfect home and set up my own perfect small business.

When I look back now from the safe distance of fourteen years, I'm grateful for the time that I spent as a prison officer, however it wasn't all a bed of roses. There were certainly a few thorny pricks that had pierced my skin.

Would I do the same thing all over again? Well, probably not, but I might've handled things a bit differently given the opportunity, especially where Joe Kerr and Donald Milne were concerned.

I occasionally meet old colleagues from Barlinnie, Glenochil and Cornton Vale and they are always quick to tell me that I was, 'very wise to get out when I did.'

'If it's that bad why don't you just leave?' I ask them.

With the benefit of hindsight, I don't think I could tolerate a job where I was so unhappy doing it, that I struggled to motivate myself to get up in the morning to attend but millions of us do this each and every day. I now adopt a different philosophy and my mantra is, 'Be the change you wish to see in the world.'

Unbeknown to me, big changes were about to happen in my life and they were about to happen fast.

My private life on the outside, which I rarely discussed openly in jail, had been delivered a devastating blow. The changes that I had sought after leaving the SPS were to change my life. They lay brewing just around the corner and were about to be dropped on my head in the most unexpected and heartless way!

Printed in Great Britain
by Amazon

36513377R00109